Samantha E. Clark

Editing, design, typesetting and publishing by UK Book Publishing

www.ukbookpublishing.com

ISBN: 978-1-916572-56-0

Contents

My Book

I'm hoping that everyone who reads my book feels enlightened and encouraged. I want you to see your own uniqueness and embrace it. I want you to draw strength from my book, have a laugh, have a cry, if you need to. Let your emotions flow with the realisations that what you are experiencing is probably normal for an autistic person. If you do things differently to me or have other quirks to me, that just makes you, you, it doesn't make you any less autistic. We are all individual and different people, and every one of our thoughts and feelings are valid.

I'd like to make a difference to all autistic people out there who are struggling and who are currently in similar situations to that which I found myself in.

I've written my book to tell my story, to share my autism-isms with you all. I want to share my uniqueness, my quirks, my weirdness, my trials and tribulations, my sadness, and the laughable things I do, that makes me, well – ME.

Writing this book has allowed me to talk to lots of people without all the social awkwardness.

My book enables me to overshare (in a good way) with no fear of it being wrong or devoid of embarrassment.

I can say for the first time in my life, I AM PROUD OF ME and who I am.

Dedication

I'd like to dedicate my book to

All the many ND people in our world, the diagnosed, the undiagnosed, the ones who know something about them is different. To the family, friends and loved ones of ND people. To the ones on the seemingly endless waiting lists who need to know they are not the only ones in the world who feel and act the way that they do, just as I did. To the ones who struggle to talk to others. To the ones who don't have a support network. To the ones who feel alone.

Introduction

21ST OF MARCH 2019

It was time to attend the pain management appointment for child 1, who had been suffering once more.

Visits to the hospital had become very frequent.

- Double break in Pars interarticularis
- Right leg abnormalities
- Headaches and Migraines
- Left temporal lobe Arteriovenous Malformation
- And now back pain.

Nobody could understand why child 1 had back pain or where it was stemming from, so it was decided to have a referral to pain management.

I entered the room and felt confused. Seated in this appointment were a doctor, a pain management therapist, a psychologist, and a nurse. I wondered why there were so many professionals here – it had never happened before.

People introduced themselves and then the Q & As started, lots of them.

By the end of the appointment, it had been agreed that child 1 could possibly be living with PTSD from an incident that had happened out in Italy in 2017.

It was decided that we would attend a seminar about pain management and afterwards we would have a follow-up appointment with the doctor.

We were also offered appointments with a psychologist to help with the suspected PTSD.

I didn't know it at the time, but this would be the start of our autism journey.

Fast forward to August 2019 and child 1 (15 at the time) started the appointments with the psychologist, at which I was also present.

In that first appointment there was so much to say, so many questions to answer, lots of note-taking and what seemed so little time.

As the weeks went by the psychologist began to ask, what I interpreted as odd questions, and not really PTSD-related.

On one of what would be one of the last sessions, I asked the psychologist why all these strange questions were being asked.

The reply was, 'Have you heard of autism?'

I think I frowned, looked at child 1, then at the psychologist and said 'yes, why'. At that point I gave my knowledge of what I understood autism to be (which wasn't much).

The reply from the psychologist was that they had specialised in PTSD for many, many years and child 1 was not showing typical signs of PTSD, and in their opinion child 1 had autism.

By the age of 16 not one 'professional' (and there had been many) had ever mentioned child 1 could possibly be autistic. The diagnosis that child 1 had been given over the years were: GAD, social and separation anxieties, and was a worrier.

I nearly fell off my chair. I was stunned, shocked, upset, my emotions were all over the place.

My response was, well if child 1 is autistic then I definitely am. It was at this point the psychologist suggested I go to my GP, tell them about the situation and ask for a referral. The psychologist also said she would speak with her colleagues who are specialists in Autism regarding child 1 and ask their opinions about our situation.

The psychologist said if child 1 isn't autistic, then they know nothing after 28 years in the job.

Me and child 1 pondered, we chatted, we relieved previous appointments, we went back 11 years to when this had all started, we talked about all the times Camhs had been in our lives, then we mulled over the words and diagnoses the 'so-called' specialist people had previously given us.

We then had to find out about autism just in case we were autistic.

I mean, no director of psychology at the children's hospital would get this wrong, would they? Or at least, that's what I hoped.

I thought I had an idea of what autism was, but I really didn't.

Dr Google became a friend, a good friend.

I scrolled through social media, and I became hyper focused (surprisingly). I then ordered a few books that had some good reviews.

I read the books, I read the online articles and I was flabbergasted; it was like most of what I was reading was about me, it could have been written about me.

I kept shoving book pages under my husband's nose and saying 'JUST READ THIS', I was rather excited but bewildered at the same time.

I started replaying my life over, the counselling that worked for about 30 seconds and never had a lasting effect, the anti-depressants I had been given, with the diagnosis of anxiety with low moods and depression.

I was totally enlightened and had a massive realisation that there's a very real possibility that I was autistic, but not just me, child 1 too. It was so much to take in. I didn't know whether to cry, scream, jump for joy... I just needed to be assessed and to get answers.

COVID, LOCKDOWN JUNE/JULY 2020

This is when the autism assessment happened for me and child 1. It was confirmed that we were both indeed Autistic. I was 42, child 1 was 16. I was ecstatic, child 1, not so much.

For me, I felt I now made sense, my life made sense, my past feelings, and emotions, now made sense. Child 1 now made sense to me too.

It was hard knowing that I was an undiagnosed adult that had brought up an undiagnosed child and it was sodding tough, ridiculously tough, but now we could move forward and get help or so I thought.

I really believed that once we were diagnosed that there would be people (autistic specialists or counsellors) who would be there to help us. How wrong was I?

The diagnosis came and then one week after, there was an hour-long follow-up appointment and that's it, no more.

It was like, here's a bombshell and it's created a great big disruption in your life, off you go and just get on with it!!!

I was unbelievably stunned.

My ASD (Autism Spectrum Disorder) diagnosis has been one of the best things that has happened to me, though admittedly it took me a while to process, to get my head around it all. I had feelings of anger and upset that we had been in professional care for years and not one single person had thought that either me or child 1 could have been autistic.

After the words from the Psychologist, 'have you heard of autism?' and 'possibly autistic', books about autism became a reference point, the help I needed whilst waiting for my diagnosis. Post-diagnosis, books were an easily accessible source of information and a welcome aid when no other help is available.

Suicide

Quick acceleration.

Long and uneven road.

Extreme emotions.

Tears streaming down my face. I'm raging, confused, frustrated, and struggling.

My brain's screaming. 'There's a tree up this road'. 'A telegraph pole'. 'A streetlight'.

I press the accelerator harder, the car kicks, adrenalin is flowing.

Just hit it, just crash, just end it. 'I'm better off not being here', 'My family is better off without me'.

Within seconds, flashes of the accident crowd my head, what people will see, how my family will feel. What if I don't succeed? What injuries will I be left with? What if I break my spine? What if I lose my legs?

With all the will and want in the world, I can't do it, I reduce the pedal power and try to regain composure.

Composure and rationality don't come, only overthinking of the argument/disagreement that has got me in such a state. It's looping. The things that were said, some awful things, I then play out scenarios. I replay, what I can remember of what I said, I didn't mean it to sound how it did.

What will I do now? How can I move on? How can I go home? Where can I go? Should I just disappear and go to a hotel and turn off my phone so then people will worry about me?

I aimlessly drive around for a while and with a heavy heart return home.

The upset, teary state may continue, or it will have changed to anger, and I become silent, and quick tempered for a few days. I don't want to talk or engage with anyone.

In the next few days, I chew it all over in my brain and try to rationalise everything I can. How can I get over this? What words can I use? How can I explain what I meant? How do I try and explain things in my head that I can't even understand? How do I begin to make normal contact again?

Previously I've hit my head on hard objects to try and ease the pain of the massive build-up of emotional intensity I'm feeling after an argument.

I haven't done it again as surprisingly, it hurts, I threw objects instead! I also start to wonder and think to myself.

> What would self-harm feel like?
>
> How would I overdose?
>
> 'I don't want to live.'

'I can't cope.'

'Why do I feel like this?'

'Why do I react like I do?'

'What are all these feelings?'

'Why am I taken out of context all the time?'

'Why don't I have friends?'

'Why do people laugh at me behind my back?'

'Nobody understands me.'

'I didn't mean it; in the way it sounded but I didn't know how else to say it or how to be better understood.'

'Why am I let down all the time?'

'Why have I been called, thick, idiot, delusional, a lunatic, a psychopath, stupid?'

'I can't explain what or why I'm feeling the way that I do.'

Before diagnosis, this was me.

I still have the odd times where it's super challenging. I still have meltdowns, I become so built up that I cannot cope with my thoughts and feelings, and I can just cry and cry.

Post-diagnosis, my suicidal thoughts are almost non-existent.

Death terrifies me and so does not being here for my family.

Finding out I am autistic has been a blessing.

I have more understanding about my mental and emotional ways, which has a positive knock-on effect in my family. We are equipped (somewhat) to deal with situations better.

Crying

What are you crying for?
You're a grown woman? Get a grip!
You're crying over this?

I feel like I have cried more than a person should cry.

I cry at seemingly small stuff. I cry when there didn't seem to be a reason to cry.

I often felt ridiculous, silly, like a child, frustrated, confused, I'd get angry at myself. As I got older, a few years before my diagnosis I used to tell myself that this is just how I was and is something that I do.

Crying is a release for me, and I just needed to accept it, however embarrassing it is. I can be seen as unstable, unbalanced and a reason for others to stay away from me.

Why does society see crying as shameful, an unacceptable emotion? It's a perfectly normal response to a range of emotions that range from deep sadness to extreme happiness and joy, and I for one will never apologise for it.

WHY I CRY.

- I cry when my feelings are extreme, and I don't know how to cope with them.
- I cry to express my emotions and to get relief.
- I cry when I get frustrated.
- I cry when someone misunderstands me, and I can't make them understand.
- I cry when I'm anxious.
- I cry when I'm in fear.
- I cry when I'm stressed.
- I cry when I'm overwhelmed.
- I cry when I'm angry.
- I cry when all my emotions are built up.
- I cry when I don't feel good enough.
- I cry when I don't feel accepted.
- I cry when I feel unloved.
- I cry with tears of relief.
- I cry that I know I'm so different to others.
- I cry that I don't fit into society.
- I cry when people don't like me, and I can't understand what I've done wrong to them.
- I cry when I feel a failure and that nothing I do is good enough.
- I cry when I feel like I've upset someone, especially my loved ones.
- I cry when I put so much effort into something and get nothing in return.
- I cry when I know I could have a done a job with a lot less effort for the same outcome.
- I cry when I reminisce.
- I cry when things are unjust.
- I cry when I talk honestly about how I feel about myself.
- I cry when I'm tired.
- I cry when I think about death.

- I cry when I'm listening to certain songs.
- I cry more when someone makes me feel insignificant because I'm crying.
- I cry when people say nice things about me.
- I cry when people show genuine care towards me.
- I cry happy tears too.

Telling me not to cry won't help, dismissing my worries won't help, telling me to calm down won't help, please don't judge me.

I need to cry; it may not seem obvious, it may seem trivial, but there's a reason for my tears, so please allow me to release whatever I need to release.

Please allow me to be me.

Counselling

It's fair to say I've had my share of counselling. I think I was 32 years old when I had my first; the last group of counselling sessions were in the early part of 2016.

In total there has been four.

The first therapy sessions I encountered were with an older chap; he was lovely. He was slight with greying hair and wore glasses.

I was terrified, I was in such a mess. I remember the queasiness, the trembling, the rapid and the nonsensical talking I was doing, my thumping heartbeat.

It was all new, it was a new room in the doctor's surgery, a new person and something I never thought I'd be doing, and I was, at that time, ashamed of it all. I was unaware what would happen or how it would happen.

I didn't want to tell anyone; it was a big deal in my mind, and I was sure I would be negatively judged.

'There's nowt up with you', 'What reasons have you got, to not cope', 'You don't need to tell a stranger your problems', were some of things I believed people would say to me.

Once in the room with the counsellor, it didn't take me long to start crying and I didn't stop, I cried the whole way through. I was utterly exhausted afterwards but I strangely, really enjoyed it and couldn't wait until my next one.

At the start of every session there were always Q&As to answer about my thoughts and feelings, including any suicidal thoughts.

'Have you had any suicidal thoughts?'

I'd reply in a confident manner that I most definitely have had suicidal thoughts and lots of them. I didn't feel ashamed or embarrassed, it's a fact and I needed help.

'Have you acted on your thoughts?' To be truthful, I was too scared to go through with suicide, and I had my children, I had to be here for them.

The six sessions that I was allowed through the NHS seem to fly by in a flash. I didn't want them to end. After the fifth session I immediately started to ruminate and struggle with my emotion that week six would be my last and I honestly didn't know how I would cope without them.

On my sixth and final session, I cried, not as much as my first session. My scores had reduced, and I felt much better, but it didn't last long.

I was diagnosed with 'Low mood, depression and anxiety' at that time and I felt I had an answer as to why my life, my emotions and relationships were the way they were. I also trusted the 'professionals' that had been assigned to help me. Just like I had trusted all the 'professionals' with child 1 who was misdiagnosed for 11 years.

I don't remember when my second and third therapy session were, but all I know I was in such a mess all over again.

The fourth and final counselling sessions were CBT based and my first introduction to anti-depressants. I ended up in these therapy sessions after a heinous incident at the last place I worked. Let's just say, it made me a total fucking mess, I've never been through anything as bad in my life. It destroyed me to the point I couldn't function, over three days, I lost 10lbs. I couldn't eat, I couldn't sleep, I couldn't stop crying. I ruminated, and I looped. I just couldn't function.

Just driving near the place nearly sent me into meltdown. My emotions were that bad that when my husband took a sick note in for me, I was shaking and would feel sick, and this was while I was sat at home. If only I had known about my autism, things may have been different. I'm pretty sure that if the company I worked for had known I was autistic they wouldn't have employed me in the first place.

These CBT sessions were my first introduction to anti-depressants.

The counselling helped for a few weeks, but I would always go back to how I was. This was because my ASD was the cause of my issues and as yet hadn't been identified or diagnosed. I suppose it's like sticking a plaster over a broken leg and hoping that it works. It treated the symptoms and not the cause.

The counsellor still concluded that I had low moods, anxiety, and depression.

It's amazing that after my diagnosis there has been no need for me to require therapy sessions or anti-depressants.

I now, somehow, don't get myself into any kind of traumatic mental or physical situations that need professional help. I mostly understand the whys and hows of my own mental state and personal being.

FACT

Anxiety is not part of the autism criteria and yet many autistic people experience high levels of anxiety. Research varies on the subject, but some figures show that as many as 40% - 50% of autistic people are diagnosed with an anxiety disorder.

What I don't understand is, if these figures are so high and autistic people have extremely high levels of anxiety, why are they not a trigger for counsellors or professionals? Even if it's not the counsellor's speciality, they could speak with colleagues or refer their clients to a different department.

Is it the levels of training they receive? Or lack of training? Is it the lack of funding?

In my own and child 1's experience with the psychologist, the training and experience made a difference.

Child 1's psychologist knew that child 1 presented with what looked like PTSD but after a few meetings realised that child 1 didn't fit the normal behavioural pattern of someone with PTSD.

By the psychologist's own admission, even though they knew about ASD it wasn't their area of expertise and they would have to converse with their colleague who was a specialist in ASD. Child 1's psychologist saw something wasn't the norm and acted on it. I will be forever grateful.

There could possibly be less need for counselling, anit-depressants and fewer suicide rates in females if the 'professionals' knew and looked for the subtle signs of autism. Maybe the 'professional' training should include autism, and what to look out for. It's better to suspect autism than misdiagnose it. For me, if I had been diagnosed earlier or properly, I wouldn't have had Neurotypical counselling, which would have worked out better.

What's the worst that can happen if a professional suspects autism and it's not? These professionals can save and have the power to change lives.

Vulnerability

Looking at myself, I didn't see a vulnerable person; to be honest I don't know what I saw, I always have had an identity crisis. Not knowing who I was or what I stood for. My life was always in question.

The first time I had anything brought to my attention was quite a few years into my current marriage. My husband used the word to describe me as 'Naïve', I got a bit defensive and upset and asked him to explain, but his description and observations of me were very accurate.

Years later, more and more would emerge about what type of person I was and what I had been through, all of which were not identified until I had my diagnosis. With my naivety came the thoughts and feelings that if people talked to me, laughed with me, appeared to like me then they couldn't or wouldn't hurt me. I never believed people (especially close loved ones at the time) would ever lie to me or use me. When these things did happen to me it was extremely difficult for me to understand. Mentally and emotionally, I didn't cope very well, I would self-analyse, self-blame and wonder what I had done wrong for such things to happen to me. As a child and into adulthood I've been talked about and laughed at. It's happened at numerous stages of my life, in various environments and not in a good way. I'm all for extracting the urine out of myself and I don't mind others doing it with me, but it's painful to know it's happened in a malicious way. Sometimes I've witnessed it with my own eyes and ears, other times people have been kind enough to let me know what's been said.

My extreme reactions, my overreactions, my meltdowns (unknown to me at the time), my weirdness, my differences, my clothes, even some backpacks that I had in my 20s, have been a focus point for ridicule. I think this is why I now have a fear of overhearing people talking, I sometimes put my fingers in my ears or make noises to block out the voices or conversations.

I can easily catastrophise about what is being said, fearing the worst. Sometimes, I will interject to stop the flow of conversation and need to know what is being said so I can feel safe and calm and that I'm not the topic of conversation.

During the time I separated from child 1's biological father to when I met my wonderful hubbie, I was lost, big time. I had been through years of hell; I had suffered mental abuse in the form of Gaslighting.

Imagine, I'm undiagnosed with a small child undiagnosed and being Gaslighted! I was, in a sense, 'fucked'. The ex was so good at what he was doing, that he even convinced my parents that I was going insane.

I didn't fully understand what had happened to me until he started doing it to his own child. It was sickening and child 1 was affected on a serious level. Child 1 is now old enough to realise and understand, can see what's happening and responds accordingly.

The 19 years of child 1's life, the fractured relationship with her biological father and to which I continued to suffer, could be a book on its own, therefore I'll stop here.

The phase between the ending of my long-term relationship and marriage, and the meeting of my new man, my mental health was poor. My decision-making and judgments meant the choices I made were not the best by any means.

I had an almost desperate need to have another man in my life. Yet I had convinced myself that I would be forever alone after being told by my ex that 'nobody will want you now, as I've left you with a child'.

I went on the hunt for men and attention. I did online dating, I went out drinking in the hope of finding someone, I targeted multiple men in the gym, and I made myself look like an idiot. I did things that I would never, ever normally do, things that are (to me) cringeworthy. Honestly, just writing about all this is making me feel nauseous.

One of these instances was a date with someone from the gym, I got completely shit faced (intoxicated) within a short space of time, so the date got cut short, he brought me home, I offered him sex. I don't know how I thought I could perform; I couldn't even function properly. He declined (I'm so thankful he did), I got out of the car and wobbled up my drive and into my house. Needless to say, I felt a huge feeling of embarrassment the next time I went into the gym.

I had sex with so many people, I had brief relationships that lasted weeks or months. I went on weekend trips with these people, I visited their families. I introduced child 1 to all these different men, which I can never forgive myself for. I did all this with people that were just not my type, some of whom were a tad undesirable too.

I just wanted attention and to be loved. For some reason, I believed that if I had sex with people from the off that I would be loved. I thought sex was how I would get what I needed, even though I wasn't keen or comfortable doing it, it just felt like the right thing to do.

When I think back on it all I was lucky that I never encountered anyone or anything dangerous – the outcome could have been very different.

THE ART OF MASKING

How can you not be confident? How can you have anxiety? You don't have low self-esteem.

I pretended and I masked well, sometimes consciously and sometimes unconsciously.

Pre-diagnosis there were many times when conversations have taken place someone at work, or the gym. I tell of my struggles with low self-esteem and confidence, or that I suffered from anxiety and lots of stress, and their facial reactions would be a picture.

They would have utter shock and disbelief written all over their face. The usual response would be, 'but you come across as someone who is so confident' or 'but you're so confident'. If only they could see into my body and mind or live with me for a period, then their opinions would soon change.

I knew how I acted wasn't really who I was, and I thought most people were like that too.

I realise I can have an air of confidence about me when I'm doing what I know or what I'm good at, but there's always the little negative voice in my head, questioning all my actions or choices.

But if you give me something new to do and it's unfamiliar, then I'm in utter panic and fall to pieces.

I have been, and I am still told that I pull myself down all the time. I suppose I have my reasons. I'll do it before anyone else can do it to me. My lack of self-confidence, my lack of self-worth, anxiety.

I am aware that my vulnerability has made it easier to have been used and abused by others and it's quite a sad realisation. I wear my heart on my sleeve, so everything I'm thinking and feeling is on show, which can make me an easy target. On the flip side I have been helped by people as they can see my upset or distress without me saying anything.

I'm not on my own, I have read somewhere that autistic people are more susceptible to different types of abuse.

I was aged about 13 years old when I had something happen that had quite a negative impact on me. I didn't speak about it for years and pushed it to the back of my mind, even though it stayed in my thoughts.

There had been a visit from two older family members, the ones we trust and care about. I can visualise it, where I'm stood and in the place it happened.

As the family members were leaving, it was time to kiss and hug them goodbye. As I innocently gave the male a kiss on the lips, he held me and pushed his tongue into my mouth and said, 'I bet you've never been kissed like that before, have you?' I stood there in shock, it was disgusting, I didn't know what to do. If I remember correctly, it was laughed off as if it was something normal, just a joke. It wasn't like that for me, and it changed the way I felt towards that person right until their passing.

Vulnerability in autism can lead to many forms of abuse, social exclusion and can have a negative effect on mental wellbeing.

Abuse is life changing for many and is something that will haunt them until the day they die. Self-blame and guilt are also a consequence of the horrific acts and it's not easy to talk about, yet it's needed. Speaking to someone close, seeing a counsellor or just talking to a stranger may just help.

We are all vulnerable in different ways and at different times, we are all unique, our vulnerability cannot be measured.

Unhelpful Thinking

It's fair to say that I seem to be gifted with many unhelpful thinking styles and it's also safe to say that most of these may stem from my anxieties.

BLACK AND WHITE THINKING

In the grey matter that is my brain, things are either black or white, right or wrong, good or bad, and I have difficulties seeing any possibilities in between, I tend to not see any grey areas.

RIGHTS AND WRONGS

Many heated debates and occasional confrontations are a result of this way of thinking. I also struggle to understand other people's ways of thinking or why they do the things that they do.

I'm like a dog with a bone: if I know there has been an injustice, to me if something is wrong, I will fight like fuck to right that wrong and I won't settle until everything is how it should be. The consequences of this are that I can become easily frustrated, suffer with extreme emotions, and ultimately have a meltdown.

My voice of reason (husband) tries to help me and says that not everything is worth a battle or getting upset over. I know he's right, but my heart and my head say otherwise.

It takes so much of my mental strength and energy to not start a challenge when something is wrong, it eats away at me.

I can't rest knowing that someone or something need to be held accountable for their errors.

I struggle also, to leave a challenge that hasn't reached a suitable outcome.

I've found a way to help resolve situations quicker when I'm struggling to get help and resolution from companies. I follow the correct procedures first, telephoning and emailing, but when that fails, I email the CEO of the said company. Usually within a matter of days I receive a response and the problem is generally rectified.

I have to say that although my autism and my unhelpful thinking causes me trauma, it also gives me drive, focus and determination to see things through.

Here's an example of my resilience and determination in one of the right and wrong problems in my life that I have used my special skills for.

This part of the story may seem a little long winded but it's totally relevant

In December 2019 we had a new main door fitted to our home. A gorgeous wine-red coloured door with an Anthracite frame. Within a few weeks the door scratched easily. I don't know what made me do this, but I pulled my thumbnail along the door to test the paint, and it marked the paint. I then tried something a bit tougher than my fingernail and again it marked.

When I initially contacted the company regarding the defect, they offered to send me out a touch up pen. Not great when I had spent lots of money on a brand-new bespoke door. I declined their offer. The company then sent the door fitter back out to do a quick investigation on the door. His findings were that there was a fault with the paintwork, he noted the defects, then dated and signed the paperwork, and gave a copy to me.

As per the law, the company must be given a chance to repair or replace the faulty item. They agreed to replace the door slab but then Covid-19 hit, and we went into lockdown.

Months went by and eventually we got the replacement, but before it was hung, I asked the fitter if the door slab paint had been tested before bringing it out to me. The answer was no. I then asked him to test the door. I asked him to run his fingernail along the paint work, he did, and it marked it straightaway. He rang the door manufacturer and was told to return the door back to the factory; another replacement was ordered.

More lockdowns halted the replacement and then I was told it was on order from a 'far away country' and was being shipped.

When it arrived, the same door fitter delivered it to us. I went through the same procedure as the last time. Had the paintwork been tested before it left the warehouse? No, it hadn't been, so I got the driver to test it again and it was still faulty.

In all this time I had been given lots of reasons why it could possibly be faulty.

- The paint must be old as it's a unique colour.
- It hadn't been painted properly.
- It hadn't been primed correctly.
- It wasn't sealed.

- There was no clear lacquer finish.

Some of these were, indeed, true.

The window and door manufacturer were now starting to become a little bit more difficult.

I had given them plenty of time and opportunity to resolve the issue and they hadn't. I was fuming, it had caused severe emotions and stress, and it was now time to escalate.

As it was a large purchase, I had used my credit card as I know I have back up insurance.

It was a long process.

After what felt like days filling in claims under section 75 of the consumer credit act 1974, the escalation was now underway.

I was asked by the Credit Card company to get an independent assessment of the door; they would pay up to a certain amount for the inspection to be carried out. This scared the shit out of me, I didn't know where to start, all my worst fears and emotions were in full swing. However, I did it. I sent off the report.

For weeks I heard nothing. I totally dislike not being kept informed. I don't mind if there's a problem, I just need to be updated as to what's happening.

For my own sanity, I telephoned the claims department. Nothing to report other than my claim has been sent to another part of the company.

Not long after I receive a letter in the post. A letter from the claims department asking me to have another independent assessment on my door.

I had already had an assessment done, why do they need another one, it had already been a trauma getting one in the first place. Ringing new people, telephoning companies, asking for something that sounds weird, arranging for them to come to my home and I DIDN'T LIKE ANY OF IT.

My emotions rise and I start to go into a meltdown. I contact my voice of reason (the husband), as usual I speed talk, not making much sense, but he understands me, and the conversation between us helps me. With my meltdown in full swing, I telephone the company. I needed to know why they had sent me another letter to do the same thing within weeks of me doing the first one, and why had so many weeks passed by, and they had seemingly not acted on my complaint?

I started to catastrophise. Had someone at the company misplaced my original documents? Had it been lost in the post? But this couldn't be as I had sent the documents by special delivery so they had to be signed for.

When a human voice answered, I rambled on, I think I must have re-iterated my whole story in about 30 seconds. My voice was elevated, and I just wanted to find out what was happening. I started to read out the letter I had received from them and said I just don't understand why the company is asking me to do something again that I've already done. Then it all became clear.

It was explained that the last independent assessment I had done was done by a company that wasn't VAT registered and the credit card company now needed an independent assessment from a company that is VAT registered.

My God, really?

I didn't see that the company needed to be VAT registered in my letter, oops. I had read my letter a few times but somehow not read it correctly. Sometimes my brain sees words and paragraphs, but I can misinterpret information. I went into instant panic.

I asked why they hadn't stated this in the first place, in the first letter. I explained about my autism, how the situation is affecting me and how the new letter is causing me angst and stress. I also questioned the need to pay another company for this new independent assessment – who would foot the bill? I was told this would have to be cleared by higher management.

The employee on the telephone asked me if I would like it noting down about my autism, I say yes.

He then asked me some questions.

The employee asked me 'how long had I had autism'. I told him in a calm manner that you don't just develop autism. Another question he asked was, 'Has anything made it worse today?' He couldn't see me, but I was smiling to myself, thinking WTAF. My reply was, 'yes, this whole situation is'. I told him that the new letter they had sent me was asking me to redo a stressful task. I also told him that, autism + environment = OUTCOME; the company at this time was the environment and my anxiety and stress were the outcome. He apologised and said the questions were provided by the company for them to ask the customers.

It wasn't the poor boy's fault.

I was taken aback by the questions asked and so decided to spend time emailing the CEO of the company regarding my recent experience with their customer service. I promptly received a phone call from a Senior Customer Service Associate and a follow up email. The chap was so lovely. He spoke in a very polite and calm manner which is always extremely helpful to me, and he understood about autism (he had a family member who is autistic – this also helps).

Below is an extract of the letter I received.

> *'I write further to your email to our CEO (name left out), dated 5 September. I'm so sorry you needed to escalate your complaint about the service you've received in relation to your dispute with (name left out). Thank you for speaking with me today. This letter confirms what we have discussed.*
>
> *I've upheld your complaint about the questions asked during your call on 2 September. Whilst the agent didn't intend to upset you, I agree his questions weren't appropriate to your condition. Thank you for bringing this to our attention. I have given him feedback and updated the notes on our system to prevent a recurrence.*
>
> *I've also upheld your complaint about us asking for a second independent assessment. I've looked into this and can confirm our policy changed after our letter dated 28 June was issued. For reasons unrelated to your claim, we've had to change our policy to ensure reports include the business's VAT.'*

I did what was asked of me and submitted all the new information. Not long after I received another letter explaining that I would be fully re-imbursed by the credit card company.

Winner, winner, chicken dinner. =)

The outcome was fair and just, but it doesn't take away that I had to fight for two years with the problem and injustice sat in my brain 24/7 until it's resolved.

There are so many little things that I pick up on all the time, and I know I can't right all wrongs. They continue to be, and I will continue to fight for what's right or wrong.

INJUSTICE

As you've just read, I don't tolerate rights and wrongs very well, but I also struggle with injustice for other people too.

A big problem I have is that I can very easily get dragged into other people's problems. I listen and get way too involved in what I believe to be an injustice.

I turn into a one-woman mission to help them in any way I can. I've spent hours, sometimes days and sometimes weeks to help them. I've made phone calls on their behalf, visited places with or for them, and generally it doesn't end well for me.

People see my passion and maybe my vulnerability and begin to tell me a somewhat exaggerated story. When I give advice or offers of help, they don't refuse. I suppose if someone is willing to do things for you or fight on your behalf, you wouldn't refuse, would you?

What eventually comes to light is that the 'so-called' victims of a 'so-called' injustice weren't really that bothered in the first place. It wasn't that big of a deal to them, or they can't be bothered anymore.

In due course I come to realise, or my husband will notice and kindly bring it to my attention.

At this point, my emotions are affected, I get really upset, I feel let down. I feel like a prize pillock. I start to torture myself and question everything I've done. I get annoyed that I've wasted my time, I then need to discuss the whole situation with my husband, over and over until I can get it resolved in my brain. It's a long hard process to recover from, lasting days, possibly weeks.

I try and think that I was doing the right thing at the right time whatever the outcome.

I understand that my autistic brain has the need to fix things and make issues/situations good again.

I now don't tend to offer much help to anyone as it's a path that mentally and physically is too hard for me.

LEVELS OF IMPORTANCE – EVERYTHING IS A PRIORITY

A great acknowledgement of my behaviour by my other half is my levels of importance.

There are daily situations that occur, from small, insignificant issues to the more serious. All these require different responses and reactions regarding how great or trivial the problem may be.

In my world everything feels quite catastrophic, and I can have an extreme reaction to things that others see as ridiculous behaviour. I struggle to differentiate, and I become hugely overwhelmed, very quickly.

I can have the same reaction to somebody crashing into my as someone spilling a drink in house. As I sit writing now, a tradesman should have arrived 1.5 hours ago and it's eating me up. I've had to change my routine, move my daily plans (which has been hard enough) and then they don't even turn up. It's driving me crazy, my thought processes are all over, I'm playing scenarios and conversations out in my head just in case they turn up or even if they don't. What am I going to do if they don't turn up? That means I need to get another tradesman here and I need to start the whole stressful process again. Plucking up the courage to speak with an unknown person, deciphering what to say, then I have to make an appointment, then I have to anticipate and countdown to when they will arrive, then I will become anxious on the day of the visit and the meeting of a new person, then I will chew over the conversation and work they have done, then I have to re-iterate all the day's happenings with me hubbie. It goes on and on.

This is how my husband views the same situation. They haven't shown up, so what, they're missing out on money – THE END.

I MUST, I HAVE TO

I give myself unrealistic expectations and time frames by telling myself that 'I must' do X, Y and Z and there's no other option than 'I have' to do it all. When I can't complete what I set out to do, I often feel a sense of guilt or failure.

FORTUNE TELLING

My mind makes me believe that I know what is going to happen in any situation or that I can tell what someone is going to say. I'm always convinced too that it's going to be something bad.

FORTY TWO

CATASTROPHISING

Catastrophising is one of my many traits – a big one. Everything is always the worst-case scenario.

If anyone says they need to speak with me or 'have a word', I instantly feel a bit queasy and momentarily I feel like I've taken a blow to my stomach. Then the brain kicks in and plays through every negative scenario why this person needs to speak with me, and it means impending doom. If it's one of my family members I keep nagging them to give me an indication of what it is they need to talk to me about. Most of the time this really helps, it calms my agitated state but then I clock watch and countdown until we have the conversation.

It can be seen to others as overreacting and a bit hysterical, I see it as debilitating, annoying as feck. I have the constant rise and fall of adrenalin all the time and it's awful, so energy draining.

Catastrophising happens to me when I see emails, messages or even when the phone rings.

My brain and body seem to always be in a heightened state of arousal so anything I deem to be negative can spiral to an insane level in seconds.

After the event that I have catastrophised about and realised it was nothing to worry about, I start to get annoyed with myself for being an idiot, I start to pull myself down. A realisation that the silly amounts of worrying and energy weren't worth it.

BEING EXTREME

This is one of my autistic traits that my husband notices that I do, and I have noticed that child 1 does this too.

I use 'extreme' words or have 'extreme' reactions, such as:

'To die for' when eating a food. It's not really to die for, is it?

'I'm disgusting', 'I'm gross' when talking about myself. I may not look my best that day or my weight might have changed, but the descriptive words I use are 'extreme'.

'It's vile' when describing a new food. To my mouth and tastebuds, it's not nice but it's probably not 'vile'.

'It's filthy or disgusting' used to describe my home, my car, social places or even me. They are usually not as bad as 'filthy' or 'disgusting'.

I can easily magnify any negatives in any situation, and I play down the positives including anything related to me.

JUDGMENTAL

Any 'normal' person will gather information and evidence and make informed choices. My brain likes to make judgments without proper evaluation, making me appear to be very judgmental at times. This includes anything to do with me.

I have the intense fear of being watched and judged by others too.

CRITICISM

It's hard for me to say it, but I don't take criticism very well. I always thought I did, but I don't think I do. My fear of getting things wrong is strong and I think that criticism compounds my low feelings about myself and the need to not upset people.

I always want to know whether I've done something good or in the correct way, and want someone to tell me so. However, if the feedback isn't positive, I start to wobble. I see all criticism as negative, even when it's constructive, mentally it's hard to deal with, causing lots of emotional problems for me.

I also feel that as my mindset is mostly negative that I see criticism in a negative way too, like being attacked.

COMPLIMENTS

How hard is it to accept a compliment? God, it's so stupidly uncomfortable for me, excruciatingly painful (there's the extreme words again).

I'm never sure how I'm supposed to respond. What is the best way to respond? Do I take it seriously? Are they being sarcastic?

Usually, the best way for me to respond is with a derogatory comment, make a sarcastic comment or pull myself down.

I sometimes ignore it, pretend I haven't heard it, or I quickly change the subject.

If my husband is with me and I've seemingly ignored someone's compliment, he'll interject and say, 'Sam, that was a compliment'.

At that point, I stutter a bit, make some excuse, and say, 'thank you'.

Thinking about it now, perhaps it could be that I have such a low opinion of myself that I don't believe someone could say nice things about me. I don't think the way I am, look or dress is worthy of a compliment.

Presently, I'm more aware when a compliment is being given but I really concentrate before responding as my default has always been to make a negative comment about myself.

PERSONALISATION

I like to think that I have control of many situations. There are times when I'm less in control than I think I am, and then, when things go wrong, I blame myself when I'm not to blame. It could be an unfortunate and complicated chain of events that cause the failure and something that is out of my control. I will still ruminate and loop with an immense sense of guilt and failure.

EMOTIONAL REASONING

When my emotions are heightened my emotional reasoning can be 'dangerous' (for want of a better word). The ability to make a rational decision becomes clouded and challenging. The greater my emotions and feelings are, the more I believe them. Physical symptoms start to grow, and situations become more and more scary, when really, most of the time there's nothing to be worried about. Being rational is not one of my strongest skills.

FORTY TWO

MEMORIES

My memory is a funny thing.

I don't have a great memory, which makes me a little bit sad. There's so much of the past that I can't remember, things that I'd love to remember about my children growing, some of my good times and the places that I have travelled to. I've been to some lovely places on holiday, but I can't name most of them, I can't tell you when I went or what I did.

I shouldn't complain as this lack of memory keeps me safe from reliving some of the traumatic events I've endured. However, like a good (or bad) horror film, there are some memories that appear in my brain like a skeleton rising from a grave, triggering some powerful emotional responses.

42

RSD

REJECTION SENSITIVITY DYSPHORIA

An extreme emotional response to either a real or perceived criticism or rejection.

Quite some time ago I saw a social media story about RSD. I didn't really take too much notice of it and didn't really look at what RSD was. However, I can remember thinking ooh that sounds like me and I just carried on scrolling through the mind numbing albeit entertaining social media shite.

Having since read about RSD and its complexities, I realise without a doubt that I suffer with it and quite badly too. It's undoubtedly negatively impacted most of my life.

I've tried to think when RSD first appeared in my life and I have no clue when it began, I just remember it always being there. It's held me back; it's affected close relationships and almost sent me insane.

Ultimately, I have been at the mercy of its symptoms.

Below are some of what RSD can look like, I've picked out the ones that are relevant to me.

Having an emotional reaction to negative judgments, criticism, or exclusion beyond what most other people feel and a struggle to cope with these feelings. Big emotions are easily triggered.

Emotional regulation is extremely difficult, it sends me into a mental tailspin with lots of intense rumination.

RSD will give you all the worst emotional feelings, but you can also feel physical pain too.

My physical pains are nausea and feeling like I've been hit with a heavy object in my stomach.

Intense feelings of anxiety, depression and hurt.

As a response to my intense feelings, I can be abrupt and come across in an angry manner when I'm not angry, I just can't regulate my emotions.

With all RSD episodes, I suffer extreme rumination and then have the feelings of guilt and stupidity. The feelings of stupidity are super strong and for me can also bring on physical symptoms.

Suicidal ideation.

Refer to the suicide chapter.

Constantly feeling judged.

I always feel like I'm being judged by others. At times it can appear that I'm paranoid.

I can be out anywhere, at the gym, out shopping, dining out, sat in the car, literally anywhere and the fear of judgment rears its ugly head.

The chatter starts in my head or occasionally I speak out loud, 'What are they looking at?', 'Why, are they looking at me?'.

I can easily become uncomfortable and annoyed that I'm the focus of someone's attention. I can't rationalise, in my head these people looking at me are criticising me, criticising my looks, my clothes, anything about me or, silly as it sounds, I feel judged on the vehicle I drive. I've come to understand that it's because I feel negative about myself as a person that I believe others must view me the same.

My imagination and reality are two very different things.

Overly perfectionistic, overly high standards of oneself

I crave perfection in all areas of my life. I want perfection from others too in the way I perceive perfection to be.

I felt by having cellulite, wrinkles, hairs showing in areas I must keep hair free, having no make-up on, my teeth not being straight, my smile being wonky, people seeing my VPL, my nails being unkempt, are all signs of imperfection and I will be viewed from others as such. I feel I will be judged negatively or criticised for such things. I think this is why when I have put on weight I want to hide or be covered up with big and baggy clothing so nobody can see my imperfections. I can hardly walk about with a bag on my head to cover my face and hair though, can I?

My home and belongings must be in order too.

Panic sets in if I know someone is coming to visit and items are out of place, generally I will have to do a proper clean, all washing and drying must be done, everything straight and tidy. At least now I won't be judged, criticised, or talked about.

Can be viewed as overly sensitive.

Yep, that's me, I can be 100% sensitive; it's not all the time though. It's quite easy for me to misinterpret a written comment or a spoken word, which can trigger my RSD. My reactions differ, I can feel annoyed, irked, upset or confusion. This is where my wonderful husband helps me get clarification.

I can often feel disliked through misinterpretation. If I feel or know someone has hurt me, I will either want to go through the problem with them piece by piece (and probably overshare and confuse matters further) to understand what I have done wrong. Or I won't want to engage with them anymore, my future life then becomes more uncomfortable with rumination and dread the next time I encounter them again.

If I make a mistake, I feel I will be negatively criticised and judged, I feel I will be seen as incompetent and not liked.

I fear what I say, do or my actions will be laughed at and judged. I have a self-esteem that rises and falls accordingly, dependent on what others' thoughts and views of myself are.

I struggle with social media because of my RSD, I'll post something, read it, then look at it again later, keep checking it and many times I will delete it. I question everything I post or reply. Getting views or likes are a way to show me that I'm accepted, I'm liked and judged in a good way. Fewer views, fewer likes mean I'm not liked, I'm being negatively judged and criticised.

I have been told that I am just being stupid, that I am overreacting and questioned why I think like I do. I severely struggle when my feelings and thoughts are dismissed or are deemed to be insignificant, which further compounds my RSD.

When trying to explain what I'm feeling or going through can come across as self-pity or as though I'm feeling sorry for myself. Comments that I've had said to me like, 'stop feeling sorry for yourself' or 'Woe is me' can cut deep. I'm not actually feeling sorry for myself.

I think my issues with criticism stems from RSD, the feelings of failures, not being good enough and rejection.

Challenges in relationships through self-sabotage.

There have been many challenges in my relationships through self-sabotage and not being understood. I didn't understand myself or what I was feeling so how can anyone else understand my thoughts and actions?

Jealousy or what can seem like jealousy is a self-sabotaging issue. This was also me, although now I know about RSD, I see things differently.

Picture this, your other half, who you love dearly, is looking at another person, they find them attractive (or so your mind is telling you). Your loved one seems to be spending more time looking at them than interacting with you; every time you look at them, they are looking at the other person. The build-up of irrational thoughts start rapidly flooding your mind and by the end of the night the scenario in your head is that an affair must be happening or will soon be happening.

I believe what happens is a result of me having a deep-seated fear of rejection. The fear of worthlessness, I'm not good enough, not pretty enough, not smart enough. I don't dress the best, I'm not the best looking and why would someone like you be with someone like me?

It is a fact that my ex-husband did trip up, slip over and accidentally stuck his dick into other females so could this be the past trauma, the past rejection that plays a big part in my RSD?

I think since what happened with my ex-husband, I have been waiting for it or expecting it to happen to me again.

Challenges happen for me in situations where times don't add up. If, for example, my husband is off out somewhere but doesn't come back in a certain time frame I begin to feel intense emotional discomfort. I will work out timings from A to B and how long it takes whilst there and then timings from B back to A. I can't rationalise and I don't think of unforeseen events. All sorts of scenarios start to play out, I can start to imagine that he's had an accident and/or possibly dead and actually start to cry.

I can only endure so much of my own mental torture before I pick up the phone and call him and then I find out everything is ok. When he answers, I will talk and get upset or I can be fairly abrupt – emotional dysregulation.

After many past disagreements or arguments, I've convinced myself countless times that he doesn't love me. How could he love someone like me, who acts and says things in the way I do?

Always feeling guilty that I've done something wrong.

This is worse for me when I don't get a response or reply from a message or email in a time frame that I deem acceptable. I don't necessarily factor in that people have lives and I'm probably not that important to them.

When the reply doesn't come or is slow coming back to me, I start to question, if I was right to send it, did I sound ok, did I make sense, did I upset them? – rumination headache. Of course, most of the time, I do get a response. I panic at first before reading it then my worries disappear and then I feel a complete and utter dickhead for worrying and ruminating in such a way.

One thing I find extremely helpful is tons of reassurance.

The reassurance may be needed for how I'm looking in my clothes, my hair, or my weight, but it could be that I need reassurance that how I have acted or how I'm currently acting is ok. It may be that I need assurance that my saxophone playing is getting better, or my gym training is getting better. I may need telling over and over how much I'm needed or loved, or that I am enough just the way I am.

RSD is just so debilitating.

Literal Thinking

'TAKING THINGS LITERALLY'.

There are so many metaphors and phrases that can be utterly confusing to an autistic mind.

Take a seat – Meaning sit down.

I don't need to take a seat, thank you, I have some at home.

Hold on – usually used in the context 'hold on a minute'.

My way of thinking, what do you want me to hold on to? And why? Through experience I know I don't need to hold on to a particular item and I know it means wait as in time.

See you later – for us in our local area, the phrase, 'see you later', can just mean goodbye, a parting phrase. When you're leaving, we turn and say, 'I'm off now, see you later'. I understand this now, but I did used to overthink about what the person meant when they said it. I'd wonder when I was seeing them again, what did they mean, why did they want to see me later?

I still tend to hang onto people's words, to which, mostly, I end up in a frustrated, angry, emotional mess. If someone says, 'I'll ring you later', 'I'll message you later', I'll get back to you later', I take them at their word and cling to it and when they don't I get anxious. I think, why say it, if you're not going to do it? I've learned that sometimes, these things are said just to be polite such as, 'we will have to meet up', 'we will have to go for a drink' and it will never happen. I'd rather people didn't say such things to me as it causes me to expend unnecessary time thinking and unnecessary emotional energy.

Having people ask me, 'How are you?' I would take this question and tell them literally how I am and overshare only to realise after that's not what they wanted to hear. It's only a recent revelation to me that, this is just pleasantries and people are not really interested in how I am. My brain thinks, 'why ask me, if you don't want to know'. I have to make a conscious effort to just say, 'I'm fine, thank you' and say nothing else.

A while back I found out I had low blood pressure; I couldn't get in to see a doctor, so I used the kit we have at home.

My low blood pressure quickly became a hyperfocus.

'I MUST DO MY BLOOD PRESSURE 2X DAILY, ONCE IN THE MORNING AND ONCE IN THE EVENING'.

I was told that electrolytes help and with the gym training I do. It would be beneficial for me to add electrolytes into my water one hour before training.

Erm, ok, I'm thinking firstly what are they? So, I google Electrolytes.

Sodium

Potassium

Chloride

Magnesium

Phosphate

My liternalness kicked in and my brain thought – how the fuck do I get all these into a drink, into one litre of water to be consumed one hour before the gym.

I can't work it out and now I'm panicking, my brain goes into overdrive with what I've just read.

'I've got issues with my blood pressure and taking electrolytes is important. I need to fix my problem and I don't understand it and don't know what to do' – so I do what I always do, ring my beloved husband.

As per usual, I'm flummoxed so I speed talk without taking a breath and go all the way around the houses before getting to my point.

Turns out there was no need to panic, you can just buy powders or tablets! Who Knew? My children do take things very literally, though child 1 has got better at understanding terminology as they've grown up, but child 2 is still in the thick of taking things literally. Here's an example.

'Mum, I can't get on BBC iPlayer in my bedroom, it's asking me for email and password.'

'Ok, use my email and I'll give you the password.'

Child 2 types in the email and then asks for the password. I say the password – literalthinking1234.

'Mum, it's not working.'

'I said try literalthinking1234 with a capital L.'

Child 2 said: 'What about the try? Should that have a capital T?'

I started laughing, I replied try isn't part of the password I was just telling you to 'try' the password with a capital L'.

****PASSWORD**** literalthinking1234, is not an actual password I use!

Child 2 spent a few weeks at school in cooking classes, and each week a list of ingredients would be brought home in preparation for the next week's lesson.

One week the school was cooking 'Bubble and Squeak'.

The ingredients included things like:

- Potatoes
- Leeks
- Cabbage
- Onion
- Garlic
- Peas
- Bacon Rashers

On the Monday I did my usual food shop, ready for the school cooking lesson on the forthcoming Wednesday.

Wednesday morning came and child 2 was preparing a packed lunch for school, which included a chicken wrap and some crisps. Child 2 lifted the crisp box out of the cupboard, looked inside then looked at me and said, 'Mum, when I said I needed bacon rashers for cooking I meant I needed the ones we keep in the fridge and not these ones!' and held up a bag of bacon rasher crisps I had bought in a multi-pack.

Yep, you guessed it, I laughed out loud.

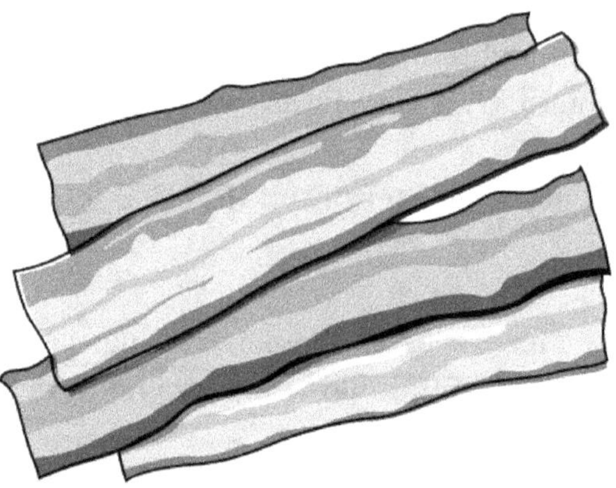

Recently, I went to watch Dirty Dancing at my local theatre with child 1. I did my usual build up to the trip out and was a bit agitated, we arrived at the entrance and the queues were HUGE!! I let out a rather large sigh and had to pick which queue to stand in. I, of course, went for the one furthest away and hoped I'd picked the one that was flowing ok.

As we got closer a member of the staff came along each of the queue lines and told all of us to have our bags open and ready for checking when we reached the entrance doors. I had on my cross-body bag and a carrier bag in my hand that contained my water, rice cakes and jam, a protein drink, and some panty liners that I had just bought from a shop.

As we neared the front, we were shouted at by the staff member who was holding their hand-held gun ready to scan our tickets. The first words were, 'Can I check your bags please?' She checked the cross-body bags and then said, 'What's in the big one?' (Meaning the carrier bag.) I opened the bag and said, 'Panty liners, water, protein drink and rice cakes.' She replied by saying, 'I didn't need to know that?' Cue my puzzled face and thoughts of, 'but you asked what was inside my bag'!

I was once in the car with child 1 and I farted, and it was a little bit stinky. I said (with a straight face) 'These drains are bad around here.' Child 1 stuck her head out the window and said, 'Yes they are, aren't they.' I burst into laughter. Child 1 looked at me and said, 'You've farted, haven't you?' I got the normal, disgruntled comment of 'MOTHER', and then we both laughed.

Rumination and Looping

RUMINATION:

- When your thoughts don't have an OFF button.
- Racing thoughts, constantly dwelling on things, can't shut my mind off, overthinking everything.

LOOPING:

We keep thinking about previous interactions and conversations (looping thoughts). There's a bit more to it but this is the relevant part for me.

RUMINATION AND LOOPING ARE:

- My arch nemesis.
- The Bluto to my Popeye.
- The Sylvester to my Tweety Pie.
- The Joker to my Batman.
- The Lex Luther to my Superman.

Rumination and Looping have got to be the things that I despise the most with my autism and anxiety. They take over, completely and utterly, they distress me, drain me, cause me to have sleepless nights and I can lose the ability to function normally. At times nearly destroying me.

My brain activity has been somewhat relentless, debilitating and the pain of it all has been so extreme, that I've wanted to rip a section of my brain out and throw it away. I just wanted peace and quiet from the relentless thoughts and subsequent emotional anguish.

It's like a hamster wheel, a washer or dryer, the thoughts in my brain go around and around and around. It may stop for a minute if I get distracted but then it's off and running again.

What I find helpful is to talk and go over anything that's ruminating or looping, I have the need to talk about the same issues multiple times but in different ways. It will be slightly different though, as I try and get a mental resolve to become calm. I need to understand the whys and wherefores of a situation or of someone's words/actions so I can process it all and come to terms with it.

Depending on the severity of the issue depends on how long it takes me to calm down or for it all to stop. It can take days, weeks, months, there have been some serious matters that happened years ago that I still ruminate over.

Even when life events go well, or I have positive experiences, I still ruminate.

The brain is a very powerful weapon. So powerful that when I'm in the throes of these toxic episodes I get physical symptoms. These can be queasiness, quivering, stomach turning like a washing machine and feeling like I've been hit in the body with a hard object, oh I forget, crying, the thing I do lots of.

Post diagnosis rumination and looping are still quite a common occurrence and hasn't really got any easier, but I now understand what is happening to me.

'If I had nothing to worry about, I would worry about not having something to worry about'.

Anxiety

Definition: A feeling of worry, fear, nervousness, or unease about something with an uncertain outcome.

For me anxiety is my autism's favourite little side kick, it's Klingon, it's the leech sucking the blood and life out of me.

Many autistic adults and children have anxiety symptoms or are diagnosed with an anxiety disorder.

Child 1 has suffered immensely with a few forms of anxiety.

Some reports state 40%– 50% of autistic adults have anxiety, others say 20%. Another report states that as many as 80% of autistic people have some form of mental health disorder. Research varies so much so it's difficult to know the true figure.

People with autism can also be affected by other mental health conditions too, such as depression, bipolar disorder, and addiction.

Anxiety is a general, umbrella term used that can describe different anxiety types. Here are some of the more common anxieties.

- GAD – Generalised anxiety disorder

- SAD – Social anxiety disorder
- OCD – obsessive compulsive disorder
- Sensory anxiety
- Separation anxiety
- Social anxiety
- Panic Disorder anxiety
- PTSD – Post traumatic stress disorder

There are a multitude of ways to help with anxiety.

First step is to see a GP if you feel able to. However, as in my experience, there will be varying levels of support.

I think it also depends on whether you have an ASD diagnosis or not. My symptoms were treated (even though they never mentioned anxiety until I asked) but there was an underlying cause of my symptoms that was missed. After receiving my diagnosis and knowing I suffer badly from anxiety, I wouldn't return to the doctors for help, I have little faith. However, child 1 has sought help for her anxiety after diagnosis, receiving counselling and medication.

The GP will be able to make a referral to a counsellor or prescribe medication.

There are apps that are available to use that are effective.

Joining groups on social media are sometimes helpful.

Mindfulness and meditation could be the key to relieving some of the anxiety.

Keeping a diary may be of use.

We are all individual and unique, therefore some treatments will be suitable for some and not appropriate for others.

It's about finding what works the best for you.

PSORIASIS

Anxiety, stress, and a bit of genetics sprinkled in triggered my skin condition called Psoriasis. I was 14 when it started – I can't think of any specific event or trauma that started it and it was odd that it began at 14.

The first step was to go to the GP and have it diagnosed and then get some topical treatment; unfortunately for me it didn't take long before it covered my body. Due to the severity of the Psoriasis, my parents said I needed to see a specialist, but I was apprehensive about going back to the doctors, but I knew I had to. The day arrived and I was called in to see the GP, I was pooping my pants.

It started off well but when I said I wanted referring to see a Dermatologist the doctor's attitude changed. This was his response: 'they will only give you what I've given you', by which he meant the topical cream. I uncomfortably stood my ground, and I got the referral I needed.

The day came to go to the hospital, and it was daunting, I'd never had to go to the hospital for anything. I remember I was at college just down the road from the hospital and would walk there, I must have been 16 or 17. I went in to see the consultant and he immediately put me on intensive treatment that I would have daily as an outpatient.

I would have to take a 10-minute bath and soak in a tar solution; it was a bit strange as the bath had to be lined with a huge, clear plastic bath liner. I then walked through an adjoining door into the small sunbed room where I had to endure UVB radiation – it would start at one minute on the first day, then two minutes the second day, the time would gradually increase. I would then walk through another adjoining door wearing my hospital gown into a larger room with beds and all shelves full of equipment.

I sat on the bed and the nurse applied a solution to my body; she started at the top and worked her way down. When an area of my body had been coated, I had to have tubular bandages over the top as a protection layer. By the end I looked like a mummy, the arm bandages were fastened to the torso bandage and the leg bandages tied to the bottom of the torso bandage. I was sent home with an ointment for my feet, I had to lather my feet in the ointment, cover with clear plastic bags and sleep in them. I had to sleep in all my bandages too. The next day I had to get in the bath and rub an oil on my body to get the residue off my skin that the nurse had applied, then return to the hospital to repeat the process. It went on for weeks.

By the end of the process my body was extremely tanned from the UVB radiation, yet I had masses of white patches up and down my body where the Psoriasis had been treated. The only comparison I can give you is that it looked a bit like the skin condition, Vitiligo.

So much for the doctor saying they would just give me topical treatment!

The treatment was fantastic, but it affected me mentally. The whole process was as scary as shit for me; every time I went to the hospital it was unsettling and unnerving. I remember that it was summer and quite warm, and I was wearing summer clothing to college, and all my patchy brown and white skin was on show. Everybody stared, comments were made, being at college was hard enough without any added extra stress factors.

Towards the end of my treatment, small bits of my psoriasis were returning but they were manageable, and it has never returned as bad as it was.

Over the years I have found a product that has really helped me: Cold pressed Flaxseed oil. It reduced the inflammation lots and my psoriasis got better.

When I first started using it, I bought the liquid form, it was like drinking olive oil, it was utterly disgusting, shuddering every time I swallowed it. I've since found the Flaxseed oil in capsules; they are now a healthy part of my routine.

What saddened me throughout all this is the guilt my dad had, he was the carrier parent of psoriasis and seeing me struggle and suffer affected him greatly. I gave him lots of reassurance and I certainly didn't blame him.

I was concerned about having my own children that I would pass it on to them, but luckily neither of them has it.

I recently found some evidence about psoriasis since my brain started to wander off and I questioned any links between autism and psoriasis. I thought I was a bit crazy – how could there ever be a link between psoriasis and autism?

Well, there is research suggests that children with autism are more likely to have psoriasis, eczema, and allergies than neurotypical children. It is suggested that women who have psoriasis or eczema are more likely to have children with autism.

I've read that one study shows that there is a significant link between autism and headaches/migraines in children. Child 1 suffers with these.

It's a bit bizarre for me to read such things. I would have never linked autism to my skin condition or that I could have autistic children because I have a skin condition!

Escapism

I struggle to switch off from almost everything that's happening in my life. I fret and worry on a ridiculous level.

Relaxing is not something I easily do. People in general tend not to understand.

'Have you tried Yoga?'

'Have you tried meditation?'

Coming from a bodybuilding background, I've never liked the look of Yoga. I mean, women who are serious about yoga look fantastic and they probably feel fantastic too.

However, I did give it a go and I found it surprisingly tough to do.

At the end of the session, it was a time to lie down, listen to music and relax, let my mind go, go with the flow, let your body go with the music, go with the waves or whatever the fuck else I had to go with. The only thing my mind was doing was talking.

It was talking about how weird it all felt, thinking I couldn't or shouldn't move or open my eyes.

OH SHIT, there's a fart brewing, I MUST squeeze my arse together, can't let the fart go, it's too quiet and I can't disguise it, thankfully I managed to hold most of it, a little bit of gas seepage did escape though. Then I'm hoping and praying it doesn't smell.

Then I start to realise that with the excitement of it all that I need to wee, and it becomes a focus. Do I really need to wee or is it the pressure in my belly due to the trapped wind?

I lay there thinking how long there was left and what happens when the class ends. I start to think about what I'm doing after the session.

I wanted to fidget so badly, I should have realised I wasn't having an MRI scan and I could move if I needed to.

Then the boredom sets in and I'm getting irritated by the 'music'. If you've done these sessions, you'll know what music I'm talking about.

The session ends and the instructor talks in a strange voice and asks everyone to come round slowly, open their eyes when ready and peel themselves off the floor.

Then came the questions: 'How was everyone feeling?' 'Did they feel relaxed?', 'Who's coming next week?'.

The responses came flooding in from the class: 'I was so relaxed I fell asleep', 'I feel amazing', 'that was wonderful'.

How do people fall asleep in these sessions?

I didn't respond, just smiled, and said thank you. I didn't return.

Mindfulness and meditation came with the CBT counselling that I had in 2016. I was in such a mess mentally and physically that I tried anything that was suggested.

I followed the instructions; I completed it all.

I tried, I really tried, and I got temporary help but it's just not for me.

One of my pleasurable 'me times' is having a bath. A bath that is red hot, full to bursting with lots of bubbles. It's not without sensory issues though. I can only use certain bubble bath, due to the smell and how it feels against my skin when I'm in the bath. If I have used a bubble bath that isn't my usual, I find the bubbles disappear quickly and then the water feels weird. I love to be in there for at least 30 minutes or until I feel my toe skin getting wrinkly – the wrinkly skin though is not my sensory friend.

I have found one way that I can shut off and relax, and it's a sunshine holiday. I don't fully relax or completely shut off, but I seem to become a different person, a better version of who I am at home.

We try and visit other places too that are not sunshine breaks, which is lovely, but my personality remains the same as home. I'm triggered by most things, sensory, emotionally and on high alert all the time, which is exhausting, and I often feel more tired when I get home.

The planning and preparation for holidays are an absolute nightmare for me. My ASD with my anxiety is awful from the day we think about booking until day 1 to maybe day 2 of the holiday.

I'm the one who books the holiday, sorts the insurance, deals with transfers, acquires the foreign currency, sorts the packing for me, the husband and child 2.

Then with my autism I have all the build up to the actual event. Prepping for the taxi to the airport, then all the issues and stress the airport and flight brings. Then the worry of the transfer to the accommodation and then getting all settled in.

Once that's done and if there are no other problems, I start to relax.

You'd think after the traumas I've experienced on my holidays, I would never have travelled again, let alone relax.

- An apartment I was in, in Lanzarote, got broken into on day 3, and most items stolen.
- In America, when I was 11, we experienced a car smash, grab and run, not necessarily smash, just open the passenger side car door, grabbed what they could out of the car and ran. Ran and dived into a convertible car and it sped off.
- Arrived at the hotel in Tunisia and had just unpacked, went to put the valuables in a safe then returned to the hotel room to find that one of our items had been stolen.

- The husband was refused to fly out to Greece on the family holiday for not having the correct Covid-19 QR code.

But in 2016 we found the most perfect place for me as an autistic and anxious adult. I've never felt so calm.

It's so tranquil, the clientele of people is perfect, the native people are fantastic too.

A few days before returning home I feel myself begin to change. My calmer personality starts to decline as I endure the build-up phase of the return journey. I don't like it.

Ideally, I want to be that person who is calmer and relaxed all the time, but it will never be. So, I'm happy to accept the times that I am able to feel some relief from my usual stresses and strains.

Come Downs

Some days – I say some as they don't happen for me very often – I will have the most fantastic day. I will get up in the morning and instantly feel better than any other day. I will feel good and it's a strange feeling to have.

Take Friday last week for example.

I got up, the sun was shining, it was lovely and warm. I went for a walk, child 2 was off school (due to the strikes) so we went to the gym. I felt happier and more confident in the gym. Child 1 was at home waiting as we were all (including my parents) going on our annual strawberry picking day. I say day, it was a few hours.

I drove to the strawberry picking farm; it looked busy which made me feel anxious, but it was ok. We laughed, we took family photos, we walked to a section where there were no other people, where there would be more strawberries too. We ate fresh strawberries, we picked lots of strawberries and then got violated when it was time to pay for them, lol. We sat as a family in their café, had drinks and ice creams then we drove home. We laughed, joked, and sang along to the music. One song 'Tequila' came on and whilst sat in traffic we wound the windows down and sang 'Tequila' at the top of our voices. I then spent a couple of hours shopping with child 1. The day was filled with simple things, but it was chuffing amazing.

What I recently discovered about myself, that when I've had one of these 'supercalifragilisticexpialidocious' days I seem to suffer the next day. It's like a 'come down', like a hangover but with no alcohol involved. I feel worn out, gloomy and grumpy, and it usually lasts all day.

How odd is it for me to say I struggle with feeling happy, it's not normal for me but I kind of like it.

Could it be that I have used a huge amount of my social battery and my body is having to slowly recharge? Could it be that I want to be happier more often and I don't know how to do it in my world of negativity?

Control

IT'S A WEIRD ONE.

I have a BIG issue with being in control over most things and yet there are times when I don't want to be in control. There are times when I'm in control and something happens, and I panic or become emotionally distressed, and I need to ask my husband to help me or completely take over.

I like to control what happens, when it happens, where it happens or how it happens.

Sometimes, if on the off chance we decide to go out somewhere (for the day or for a meal), it feels like the biggest decision of my life, and I don't want to choose, I don't want to be in control. The choices are too overwhelming. At this point my husband starts to make suggestions and my inner Andy (Little Britain) comes out, 'DON'T LIKE IT'.

Decision-making can easily lead to me having a meltdown, having to make a choice can become overwhelming and frustrating.

Since my diagnosis and trying to understand myself, I think the control is a safety and comfort thing.

What I mean by safe is, safe from anxiety and stress, it keeps me in my comfort zone, and it allows me to keep myself calm the best way I can. Unknown environmental factors, people's reactions, people's ways, or decisions, can quickly unsettle me and throw me into an absolute tizzy.

I need my home clean and tidy in a certain way to be able to feel calm and relaxed too.

Having 'a daily routine' is what I need; if I change something in my daily routine, that's ok; if a person or unforeseen event causes changes to my routine it causes me so many problems and is very unsettling.

When appointments are cancelled, when times of upcoming events change, when I'm needed to alter my routine at the last minute, I lose all sense of control, and I struggle to cope. I can get really agitated, I struggle to control my emotions, or I can go silent and become sharp and snappy to anyone around me. I can become silent while I try to rationalise and deal with what's happening in my own way.

My mum, the undiagnosed autistic, has had a severe control issue all her life, growing up I hated it and didn't understand it AT ALL. My mum's reactions to things when her control was questioned or taken away was horrific, so extreme, it wasn't nice to be around. Growing up I was kept close; I was over protected. My mum took care of me in the way her own upbringing and her own past traumas allowed her to. Today, I am so much more aware and understanding of why she reacts the way she does, says the things she says and her mannerisms.

I fear the unknown, I need to know what's happening, sometimes I feel it's best to be informed. Forewarned is forearmed.

I'm always asking my kids and my husband question after question, who they're messaging, the context of conversations, I need their phone calls to be relayed back to me. This is especially difficult for me and those around me.

Selfishness

I don't like selfish people, but I am one and I know now why and it's not intentional.

Before my diagnosis I had been told I was selfish at which point I would get defensive as I hated anyone saying I could be selfish. My thoughts would go to other selfish people, how they acted, and I knew I wasn't like them. Therefore, how could I be selfish?

I'm selfish in my own autistic way, things must be my way, the controlled way, my routine way, things done in a way that I am comfortable with.

I can be very emotionally distracted or upset by the things that make my life ridiculously uncomfortable, therefore I'm not going to do anything that would make my life even more uncomfortable, why would I?

I am loving (in my way).

I am kind (in my own way).

I love and care for others (in my own way).

I make sure I wash, cook, and clean for all my family.

One of my fixations is the gym (more on this later). I have a routine and I must go unless I'm physically unable (that's not true either as I've hardly been able to walk at times, been in extreme pain and still gone to the gym).

When the kids were younger and they got ill or I had to pick them up from school early and it interrupted my plans , I'd get pissed off, not at them but at the situation. My routine had changed and it would feel like my world was ending.

Now we're older and we have our diagnosis, I understand the way I act and feel the way I do. When things change, I now don't think it's the end of the world. It's still mentally and emotionally challenging but more bearable.

I get sarcastic comments from my family such a lot because I can often make myself a hot drink and not ask anybody else if they want one. I will get myself a snack and not ask if anybody else wants one.

It does irk me though if a member of my family doesn't ask me if I want anything whilst they are getting their own!

I have learned that it's not a premeditated selfishness, it's just trouble perceiving the feelings of others and lack of consideration of thoughts and feelings of others outside of our own.

Has anyone talking with someone with autism noticed that in conversations and discussions the talking point always seems to lead back to them?

It's like the song by McFly, 'It's all about you'.

To be honest, child 1 does this so much and we often say, 'it's not about you' or 'we weren't talking about you'.

I do notice myself doing it and I can imagine what the other person(s) must be thinking when I set off on a rant.

I've done it myself when I'm talking with someone and all they want to do is talk about 'themselves' and I think to myself, you're an absolute tit and I try not to talk to them again (if I can help it).

Empathy

I can be very empathic, just not in a what would be classed as a normal way. I didn't realise how different my empathy was until child 1 and I had a talk.

Child 1 told me that there was lack of emotional support from me as a parent through the childhood years. Child 1 explained that after our diagnosis, the way I was as a parent all made sense. It hit me hard. I truly believed I did show empathy in a normal way but the normal way for me was an autistic way and not a neurotypical way.

I'll try and explain.

I don't have much compassion or patience in many situations.

I can't share what someone is feeling, yet if I can physically see a problem, I'm greatly affected by it.

My eyes and empathy only see the physical problems.

When child 1 had brain surgery, I was massively affected.

Before the diagnosis when child 1 had a panic attack or a bit of a meltdown, I was quite cold, quite harsh. I was uneducated and didn't know any better.

When I see my family hurt or upset, my stomach churns and I don't really know what to do. I'm thrown into chaos; I sometimes react in ways I think I should react or how I've seen others deal with similar situations. In my later chapter 'hugs' you'll see how hard it is for me and this can be as hard with my own family. Many times, when child 1 has been upset, my response is a blunt 'oh'.

There have been times when my children have come home from school and have been upset. My default mode is 'I must fix it' and this is my empathy to the situation. Child 1 has described that all that was needed was a soft voice, a cuddle, a calm and quiet chat, and I go full-on tactical soldier approach. I'm not calm, my voice elevates. I must find out every detail of the situation and then go off and 'fix it', whatever it takes.

On the flip side, I can cry very easily at random shit.

My empathy can be shown by relating to other stories when they are talking about themselves or their lives.

Happy and Positive

Just isn't me, but I do try.

I'm in awe of these happy-go-lucky people who are always cheerful and smile all the time.

I seem to be a negative Nelly (whoever Nelly is).

I always have been, probably always will be.

As much as I try to be positive it's just not there. I think, perhaps, it's my constant overload, being frequently overwhelmed, fearful, anxious or my worrying over everything that puts a block on being happy.

Tiredness doesn't do me any favours either, it increases my negativity; in fact, everything is worse when I'm tired.

It can be a very dark and unhappy place, not just for me but for the others around me.

Have you ever heard the saying, 'there's always someone worse off than you', it's a saying that my parents and my husband like to use and to be honest I've said it to others.

I understand the saying and I get the fact that there are hundreds and thousands of people worse off than me, but it makes no difference to how I feel or think.

I've been berated for being negative. I always see what is wrong in a situation or what hasn't been done, as opposed to what is right or what has been done.

I'm stupidly negative about me as a person too, I pull myself to bits all the time, the way I talk, look, walk, act. There's no worse critic of me than me.

When I think I've done something good or worthwhile, it's very often short-lived. I play things down, down to a level that I feel comfortable with. What's strange though is that maybe a few days afterwards, I'll think about what I've done and feel a massive sense of achievement and pride.

An example:

Ancestry – 2022. I found four unknown biological fathers as a novice.

I helped people, I gave them something nobody else could do, without them employing experts and paying thousands of pounds for the privilege.

Some of the family members I did this for had wondered all their life where they came from, what their birth name should have been and did they have any more family out there.

I selfishly researched and gave my time to do this for them. In doing so, I ended a need and want in their lives that they so desperately longed for.

With my help I found and introduced them to their new family members.

The new families couldn't believe it.

It meant everything to the individuals that I helped, but to me it was just something I did. I wondered what all the hype was about.

Afterwards, every now and again, I would watch an episode of Long-lost family or DNA family secrets and I would cry. I would feel a sense of overwhelming pride that I had done this for my family, and I had changed people's lives forever.

SMILE – YOU'RE ON CAMERA

The issue with my lack of self-worth and inability to accept and like me for me morphs into a few areas, and having photographs taken is one of them.

It's so bloody uncomfortable and difficult.

Have you ever seen the 'Friends' episode. The one with 'Chandler can't smile'.

Yep, that's me.

My mum and child 2 are the same as me. I find it quite hilarious watching them both pose for pictures.

The best photos are the ones taken on the sly, the ones taken without prior knowledge or planning, the ones without the anxiousness of not knowing WTF to do with oneself. Not knowing how to stand, where to put body parts, do I show my teeth or not, maybe it's best not to as my teeth are quite yellow and not straight.

It doesn't help when my mother (in her autistic honesty) after seeing a photo I posted online says, 'your teeth look bad, I didn't think they were that bad, you need to get them sorted!'!

I'm currently having to take videos of myself training, to send to my coach.

Firstly, I find taking the videos not natural, I'm aware it's what most people do in today's world, but I find it awkward.

I'm then forced to watch myself in my video so I can edit it. It's so cringeworthy. I wince and pull myself to pieces. Mentally I try hard to not pick up on every negative little detail about me that I find and just do the job at hand.

Some days I can be quite elated with the way I look, and I get an elated feeling and want to share it with the world. I share it on social media and then I instantly regret it.

I think that may be my attention to detail, my overthinking, my negative thoughts that cause the issues, but who knows?

By the way does it ever get any easier?

At what point in your life do you not care about how you look and feel? At what point do you not give a rat's ass what anyone else thinks?

Contradictions

I like to be on my own and doing my own things, and be in control, but at the same time, I can feel very lonely and...

need to know someone is there for me.

I can happily not communicate with anyone for days but then I get an overwhelming urge to not feel alone and...

I need to know someone is there.

From time to time, I want to be on my own but don't want to be alone. I need someone around me or near, but please, don't talk to me or don't come near me but...

I like to know someone is there.

Every now and then, I need a quiet, empty house but...

I need to know someone is there if I need them.

I need to be held or hugged but on my terms.

Hug me – but not for too long, that's enough now.

Hold me – not too tight, that's enough now.

But...

I need to feel someone is there and that I am loved.

I have times when I've had enough of being in the house, I feel suffocated, I need to escape, but I don't want to go out. There are times when the more I stay in the house, the less I want to leave it.

The outside world feels scary and doing the 'peopling' thing is too much to cope with.

Sometime the fear wins.

Other times, when I don't overthink things and I venture outside, I have enjoyed it. It's been the tonic that I have needed.

However, there's no place like home.

I can be anti-social, yet sociable.

I may struggle to start a conversation, but I can talk the hind legs off a donkey.

Certain days I can be irritating and chat too much, other days I just keep my head down and don't want to talk.

I can get emotionally distressed if I don't want to be sociable and it's forced upon me, but if I have no choice but to socialise it can help my mindset.

It's fecking crazy.

Inconsistencies

One thing about my autism that my husband has struggled to understand is my inconsistencies. How I can react very differently to what seems to be the same event or situation.

I can be at ease with a situation one day, with little anxiety and stress, then another day – BOOM, I'm in utter panic, having a meltdown.

He asked me why this is, and I couldn't give him a reason.

By researching and reading I think I've found the answer.

I wake up safe to the safety and comfort of my home and throughout the days I'm walking out to an ever-changing physical environment. Situations that are out of my control. My mental state is constantly changing to accommodate this, and this impacts how I respond to what is happening around me.

I'm stepping out into the unknown, the uncertainty is scary.

Other people's mannerisms, body language, their actions and reactions are forever changing, therefore can impact my actions and reactions.

A few examples of my possible day-to-day changes.

THE GYM

Will it be busier than normal? Will there be new members? Will there be different people in today? Will the parking be an issue for me?

THE SUPERMARKET

The car park is having some alterations. I can't park where I normally park, where do I go, what do I do?

The usual customer assistants are not working today. There are different people working on the tills.

The consumables have been moved around in the shop. The shop is busier than normal. Some of my usual groceries are out of stock. Some of the products that I buy are discontinued.

DRIVING

My normal drive is interrupted.

There are accidents, road works, causing diversions or queues. I have to deal with other people's dubious driving skills.

MY TELEPHONE

Someone is trying to phone me.

Who is it? I don't recognise the number. Do I know them? Shall I answer? Will they be polite? Will they understand me?

It's an ever-changing environment. If the situations never altered, if people's behaviours stayed the same, it would make my life so much easier to deal with, but it can't and it won't.

AUTISM + ENVIRONMENT = OUTCOME

I love this saying.

For me and my experiences, the saying is 100% true.

I suppose my autism can seem to be a whole heap of anxiety when things are not quite right but when everything in my world is right – I AM HAPPY, I AM CONTENT.

HUGS

GOOD GOD – HUGS

It's ALL just so weird.

I hated hugs and close contact as a child and not much has changed.

'Brace yourself, Sam, there's a hug coming.'

Why is it hard and uncomfortable to hug, it's so awkward and weird.

You just know when you've met up with family or acquaintances and it's getting close to parting ways (thank fuck for that), it will be THAT time, the time the arms are extended and put around another person.

My brain senses it way before any sort of hugging commences and my emotional uneasiness starts, then I can't focus on anything else.

Everyone stands up.

If I'm feeling brave, I'll get in there first to get it over and done with. If I'm a bit all over and not very sociable, I will move out of the way or look around or busy myself until, 'SAM, YOU REALLY NEED TO DO THIS' is in my head.

It may be just me but then I start to drive myself nuts with how I just acted in that moment and how I was perceived.

In the few seconds of a hug, I notice whether people smell, are they wearing perfume? Aftershave? Do they smell of sweat? Chip fat? Or haven't washed in a while or 'ooh, what's that fabric softener they use'.

I feel their lumps and bumps, how round their belly is when pressing against me, have they got a bra on, where their boobs are located, have their boobs gone sideways with age?

There are many days when I just don't want anyone to come near me, let alone hug me. I have found though that it's easier to go through the motions of hugging and just do it rather than cause any upset. Albeit, for them it might be like they're hugging a piece of wood.

I say this through experience, the experience of me speaking out, of not wanting to be hugged or touched and having the other person react in an unpleasant way, which has happened. I then have to live with the feelings that I've offended someone and/or they think I'm really odd.

In the past I have been known to hug someone as I know it's the thing to do at that time (when they are upset) and what that person is needing. I assume they need it; they've got one whether they wanted it or not.

What doesn't make sense to me is that there are times when I crave a hug but only from my husband. When I'm in a bit of a mental or emotional state, he wraps his long arms and big body around me and I feel safe, very safe.

Personal Space

Why is it that the general population have no idea what personal space is?

Why is it that while in a queue people want to stand as close to you as possible so you can feel their breath on your neck? They can't get any further forward by rubbing themselves against you or their bags poking your body so why do they do it? In my own experience in supermarket queues, other shoppers have nudged me or leaned over me to get their shopping on the till belt – So RUDE.

When I get to the tills, my anxiety goes up, I feel more alert and much more uncomfortable.

Here's a few things I have learned over the years to help combat the lack of personal space.

1. When you know someone is very close, take one foot and step backwards, don't say anything.
2. I've asked someone if they would like a cuddle, when they questioned what I said, I told them I thought they would like one as they were that close to me.
3. Get out your phone. Open your music then start to play 'Don't stand so close to me' (by the Police), very loudly.
4. When nudged with bags or bodies just to get an inch further on the conveyor belt, shoot them a nasty fecking look. Normally the response is 'oh, I'm sorry', just fuck off, Karen.

It doesn't stop it happening but it helps every now and then.

Covid-19 was pretty cack, but to be honest, I quite liked it. I liked it because people had to keep their distance and that it was quiet on the roads and in shops.

Communication

I'm not blessed with the 'gift of the gab', communication is not one of my strongest points and I find it quite challenging.

SPEAKING

I tend to not finish my sentences; do I know why? I haven't got a clue. All I know is that it's brought to my attention very frequently by my close family.

I'll start a sentence, 'would you mind?' and then I'll get distracted or start watching something else or doing something else or talking to someone else, and don't finish what I'm saying. A sarcastic comment will be given by child 1 or the husband – 'would you mind...!, finishing your sentence?'!

Child number 1 thinks I'm incapable of answering a question with a single answer too. When a single answer is all that's required, I tend to answer the question with a question... I have lots of ifs, buts and maybes that I need answering in my mind before I can answer the question put before me.

I'm not very good with social cues either. It can appear to others, when I butt in, that what I have to say is more important than what they have to say, but it's not.

I Interject in conversations when others are talking and I think I've realised why.

When chatting, something of relevance will come into my head and often I won't be able to continue concentrating on what's being said by others because I need to get out what I need to say. All I can think is that 'if I don't speak now, I'm going to forget what I need to say', and the 'I've just had a thought appear in my mind and it needs to come out of my mouth right now'.

There's the inappropriate talk too that I do, the innuendos, the sarcasm. However, only with my close family do I blurt out ALL that I'm thinking, as otherwise if it was said out loud in the presence of others I would be in SO much trouble.

Child 1 often says with utter dismay 'MOTHER' when I come out with something she deems inappropriate.

BRAIN TO MOUTH – NO FILTER.

I was out shopping with child 1 around November time, buying Christmas presents. I wanted to buy child 2 a new silver chain so the search was on. After looking in multiple shop windows we came across Beaverbrook's; they appeared to have some lovely items for sale.

Shopping is hard enough for me and what I really don't like is as soon as you walk into a shop the staff instantly ask what you're looking for, how can they help, blah, blah, blah. I don't want to be bothered, I need to try and focus and look around for myself and then if I need any help, I will ask for it. I kind of want to appear invisible until I need to be seen (if that makes sense).

I was hesitant to enter Beaverbrooks as the staff were stood around almost ready to pounce on us, but we went in anyway. We didn't get jumped on as I thought we would, we just got lots of staff smiles. We looked at the items for sale and found something that I thought was ideal for child 2. The lovely lady asked us to take a seat and asked if we would like a drink. Me and child 1 looked at each other with raised eyebrows and a smile. We're not used to service like this.. We were offered prosecco, gin and tonic, or a cup of tea. I kindly accepted the offer of tea as I was driving, but how nice was the service? I enquired about buying a watch too for child 2 and another lovely staff member joined us. I think there were three at one point.

We drank our tea and made our decision on what we were buying.

As we sat and chatted, the employees began to wrap the necklace. It was put into a large box and then out came the tissue paper and a snazzy paper gift bag and posh ribbon to fasten the bag. At this point I remarked how their gift wrapping resembled the scene from the film 'Love Actually' when Alan Rickman is buying the necklace for his bit on the side and Rowan Atkinson is gift wrapping it in the department store.

Me, child 1 and the employees began talking about 'Love Actually' and how could Alan Rickman's character could do such a thing to his wife played by Emma Thompson. One employee said she didn't know what the character 'Mia' saw in Alan Rickman's character, Harry. She remarked that Alan Rickman must have had a lot of money (implying she was a gold-digger), and my response was 'or he had a BIG COCK'. It just came out, no thoughts, no filter, it just came out. There was a fit of laughing from the employees as obviously they're not used to their customers saying such a thing.

Child 1 did laugh and then afterwards said, 'I can't believe you said that, Mother!' Neither can I kidda, neither can I.

It was a shopping trip to never be forgotten.

UPSETTING OTHERS

I'm quite a sensitive soul and I'm greatly affected when I feel like I've upset someone.

I never get out of bed in the morning and think, 'right today I'm going to upset or distress someone'. It's not in my personality, I'm not naturally a mean or unfavourable person. But it always seems to happen.

All my life I have been taken out of context, misunderstood. It happens even when I'm trying to be nice and positive.

It's a fact that, what's in my head is probably going to come out of my mouth.

It could be that I don't know where my social boundaries are. It could be my RB face and my glaring eyes when I talk. It could be the other person's body language when I'm talking to them or the tone and choice of words they use when responding to me. Could it be my (at times) brutal honesty?

I can play a conversation over and over in my head , but it still comes out all wrong. It's a normal thing for me to have to try and explain what I meant to a person/s, and in what way I meant to say whatever I was saying. Most of the time my over-explaining leads me to dig a deeper hole for myself, to overshare more or to overcomplicate matters further.

If I feel like I've upset someone or someone makes it apparent that I've upset someone, just know that I will be thinking about it every night for the next BILLION YEARS!! Oh, and just so you know, it'll make me feel physically ill too.

If I sense that I've upset someone, looping and rumination will ensue.

I talk it over and over with any one of my immediate family. Did I say this or that correctly? Did I come across in a certain way? Why did the person react the way they did? Should I have said what I said in a different way? Did I sound harsh? Was I blunt? Was I too honest? Why did they respond in that manner?

It's all very emotionally exhausting but now I understand my autism, this part of my life makes sense.

I really dislike having to see or speak to someone, knowing I may have upset them or there is ill feeling between us. I never know how to act or what to say and the build-up is horrendous. I always want to revisit what's happened with the person and try to explain my words or actions just to make sure we understand each other and in the hope that everything will be ok. I also realise that I try and overcompensate and act over the top with the person. It's my way of creating the emotional feeling of calm and peace within, something I crave.

Another 'special skill' me and child 1 share (I say with a smile) is the ability to talk fast. It's not all the time, though I tend to do it when I'm anxious or in a heightened state emotionally. When this happens, my husband looks at me and says, 'AND BREATHE'.

OFFLOADING

Oh my, I'm super good at this one.

I'm super lucky that my husband can talk to me throughout his workday. Most days, I need to speak with him while he's in work to rid myself of whatever I'm experiencing. It really does help to relieve my brain, slowly and steadily of its overload. If I can't speak to him throughout the day, his ears are in for it when he gets home from work. All the daily events, traumas, telephone calls I've had will be released at the speed of a travelling bullet straight in his direction before he's even taken his shoes off. That's when I get, 'Sam, I've just got in, can I at least take my shoes off'.

It's a trauma though when I have to attend any sort of appointment.I get worked up and just talk, all sorts of nonsense comes out. Then afterwards, I think to myself what on earth did I say that for? I do tell the person I'm with that I'm autistic, so it explains my behaviour and my weirdness. I shouldn't feel the need to explain but I'd rather people know there's a reason for my actions.

In fact, explaining I'm autistic generally means nothing as most people I meet haven't got a clue what autism is, and my breath is wasted.

I'm no good with 'posh people' either. I'm too down to earth, honest, and unrefined.

I know for others, communicating with me can seem difficult at times. I'm random, I'm irrelevant and can appear blank or ignorant when a response is needed.

Quite often I have a time lag where my brain is trying to process what is being said to me so I can't reply instantly. Then there's a time delay as I think of what to say in return or how I need to act. I appear to be a bit like when the internet lags, the small circle is spinning for a while before connection is re-established.

COPYING

It can be an autistic 'thing' to mimic other people's mannerisms, noises, words, and phrases.

Quite often I'm stuck for conversation.

Small talk can be a struggle unless it's something that's an interest of mine or about me or my family.

It wasn't until my diagnosis that I realised I copy sayings and phrases; I think I do it as I am unable to think of things to say.

If I hear an expression, a joke or a witty comment being used and it gets a good reaction, a smile or laugh, then I'll use it in the future.

It helps me in the art of conversation – there's nothing worse than awkward breaks or silences whilst talking to someone.

I think, for me, it's a type of masking behaviour. I am viewed differently, seen as comical, seen as ok, therefore helping my anxiety.

STORY TELLING

'Will you just get on with it', 'Are you going to get to the point?', 'Have you finished yet?'.

Yep, it can be painful to those who listen to me tell a story of a daily event or when I re-iterate a conversation.

In my head I'm thinking, I'll be quick and the next thing you know the person I'm talking to has fallen asleep. (Not really, but you get the idea.)

Once I start to tell my tale it's a bit like spaghetti junction, I'm all over the place. I can't miss any details. I also drift off to a semi-related side story but then I explain why that piece of information is relevant.

I try not to confuse anybody by explaining each little part of the story in detail but by doing so I get them more confused.

It has been known that when I'm telling my story, I get so engrossed in the semi-related side stories that I lose my train of thought and can't finish the original story. Much to my annoyance.

ALTERED EMOTIONAL AWARENESS.

Altered emotional awareness is a big symptom of my autism that alters the way I express my feelings and saying 'I love you' is a super hard phrase for me to say.

I will copy people when they say it to me, and I will return it. I can say it, but when I feel I'm able to or I feel the situation needs it. In my past I have said 'I love you' for the person to say it back to me so I know I'm wanted and cared for.

LISTENING

I always thought I was a good listener; I am to a point but I can and often do zone out and I misunderstand what has been said.

My strong point is asking questions to understand whatever I didn't understand or got wrong.

There are times when I think I've understood someone's instructions and agree that I have understood but then I realise I haven't and start asking questions again, leading the person I'm listening to, to become annoyed at me. In my defence, I thought I did understand but then I realised, I didn't.

READING

I'm not keen on reading, I would say I don't like it and many autistic people have difficulty with comprehension.

Emails – I find lots of information overwhelming and either don't read it or scan over it and miss parts. I very frequently misunderstand them too.

Companies be like, have you read the terms and conditions? Yes absolutely!? (Said sarcastically.) Not really as I need to be a solicitor to read and understand even the first line of said 'terms and conditions'.

Emails and messages cause me so much anxiety. I panic when I see a notification that I have an email, my stomach churns and I can feel physically sick, I even start to tremble. Generally, there's nothing to worry about and then I feel a bit daft. Messages can have the same effect on me.

I like reading certain books but concentrating on what I'm reading takes some doing and I have to really focus; it's quite frustrating when I've moved down a paragraph or page and I haven't digested any of it. Here's what happens: I'm happily reading along then:

My thoughts go off on a wander about the tasks I'm doing tomorrow, or I start to maybe revisit a conversation I've had with someone, or start laughing at a joke I've previously read, or start to over catastrophise about an upcoming event.

Shit, I need to read that section again. It happens once more.

Shit, I need to read that section again. Eventually I take it in.

How do people read quickly? And how do they instantly absorb information? I'm jealous.

WRITING

I'm not great at it. When I did my GCSEs, I got better marks in French and German than I did English, don't know how that works. Is it my 'special autism ability'?

Sending and receiving text messages can be awkward and confusing to me and the other person. I've gotten myself into a right old mess with messages. My communication breaks down because I write in the way my brain is talking and thinking, which isn't the best. Therefore, what I send in messages can be unclear or be read in the way it wasn't intended.

COMMUNICATION FRUSTRATION

One humongous problem I have with communication is other people's communication with me.

When I send a message, I expect a response quickly.

Most folk in today's world have a phone in their hands or near to them most of the time, therefore I don't understand how they fail to respond.

Emails. I expect an email response within a day or two.

If I speak with someone on the telephone and they say they will call me straight back or on a certain day or time, I expect them to honour what they've said. Or they call you, leave a message and you phone back, and they don't answer.

I recently received a postcard letter saying I urgently needed to call a company regarding an issue with my home. I rang the company immediately, the lady on the phone said, 'I'm sorry there's no-one here from that department at the minute, can I take your details, and someone will call you back'. A week passed and I hadn't heard from them, so I chased it up. Can't have been that urgent, can it?

Poor or lack of communication can affect me quite significantly, I'll try and explain.

Take the above example, I need to call the company immediately, it's urgent. I panic, my anxiety and stress levels are increased, my mind starts to think about all possible scenarios, and I begin to worry. I then become highly frustrated that there's no-one to speak to and left in limbo wondering if and when I will receive a call back. In the end, the outcome was that there was a glitch in their system meaning I received a card when I shouldn't have.

If I've sent a message to someone and a reply is needed, I will look at my phone constantly until I receive it. The more time ticks by without a response, the more negative thought processes take over. I go into overdrive, thinking of all the reasons why the person isn't responding; it's not pleasant, it drives me crazy.

Usually there's a perfectly rational reason for the lateness of responding.

With emails and phone calls, I count. For example, I count how many days or weeks it's been since I wrote and sent the email and then I plan how long to leave it before sending another and/or escalating it. I then count down the days until I make contact again.

With phone calls I count the time down to when I should be receiving the call, for example, it's three hours until they call me, now it's two hours, now it's one hour, it's 30 minutes, it's 15 minutes, etc, then I start to make sure I have my phone on loud and carry it everywhere with me, even to use the toilet as I can't miss the call.

If the person calling me is late, I count again. It all becomes a fixation.

'It's been five minutes since they should have called, they are now ten minutes late, it's been 15 minutes, 20 minutes.' It goes on and on until they get in touch.

As you can see it's all anxiety and stress, waiting and waiting for the call.

There was an appointment made for me to speak to a customer service advisor at 14:00, she didn't call until I emailed her at 15:00 asking her if she had rearranged our time and hadn't told me. I had sat at my computer from 13:45 waiting and didn't move. The documents that I needed to discuss with her were on my PC, so I sat there very, very impatiently.

Physical appointments are just as crazy – me and child 1 once sat waiting for an appointment and it ended up being one and a half hours late. I was climbing the walls, and when we were shouted in for the appointment I was raging. Child 1 said I nearly made the doctor cry. This wasn't my intention, I was just mentally and emotionally overloaded with frustration. If we arrived one and a half hours late for the appointment, they wouldn't see us. Why can't staff update everyone on what's happening?

Why are people like this?

My husband frequently tells me that I shouldn't expect others to behave and act how I act.

It seems to me that today, in society, many people just don't care how their actions affect others. I find it disappointing, and it makes my life as an autistic so much more difficult.

Common Sense

'COMPUTER SAYS NO' (LITTLE BRITAIN QUOTE)

I'm quite intelligent and I have some great skills, and talents, but don't really have much common sense.

Me and my family laugh at my lack of common sense sometimes until it hurts.

The looks I get from my family when I say or ask anything are something else. It's the look of WTF is she going to say now face!

Quite often my husband says that he lives in the Twilight zone.

I have a habit of saying something that has no connection to the conversation we are having. My husband will look behind curtains, underneath the cushions or seats, I ask him what he's doing. He tells me he's looking for the relevance of what I've just said.

In my head I know why it's relevant, I just have to try and explain to him why my thought process led to that outburst.

I'm the annoying one who asks lots of question when watching TV or films.

Me and the husband were once watching a documentary on 'Jack the Ripper', I asked him how they knew his name was Jack? To which his response was to belly laugh.

Whilst watching the Queen's funeral procession, I began asking questions about the Pallbearers. I turned to my husband, referencing the pallbearers and asked about their 'Fezzes' on their heads.

Hubbie shoots me a look and says,

'Did you just say, Fez?' and falls into a fit of giggles and does a Tommy Cooper impression.

I learned that day that what the Queen's pallbearers wear on their heads are a Busby and not a Fez.

Every day is a school day.

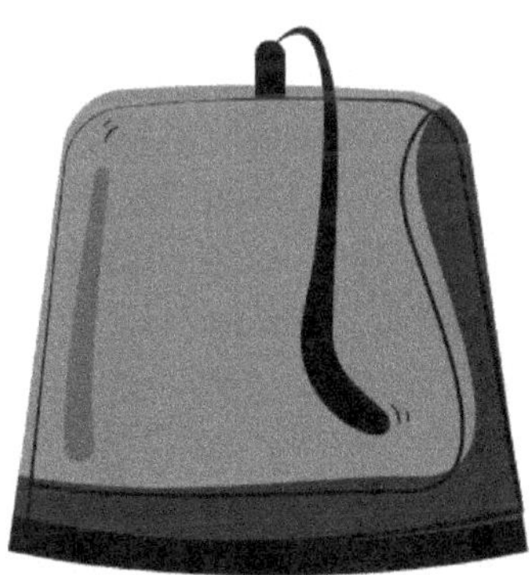

One day me and my husband were relaxing in the front room and child 1 walks in saying it'scold and does the house feel cold to us?

I had to agree, the house did feel cold, and child 1's response was 'but it's too early in the year to put the heating on, isn't it?'.

I respond with, 'It's ok, we're generating free electricity through our solar panels.'

As soon as the words left my mouth I did a Homer Simpson – DOH!!!! Cue the family laughing. The heating for our home is run on gas, not electric. Oh dear!

One weekend morning me and the husband are drinking coffee in bed, and he asks me about my previous night's sleep and how I'm feeling.

'Do you have a headache this morning?' he asks.

Me: 'No, but my eyes are stinging a bit, maybe it's because I need to get up and do some stuff, busy myself'.

The husband looks at me and raises his eyebrows and falls into a fit of laughter and says,

'So, doing stuff will stop your eyes stinging, will it? WTF, Sam!'

Then I start laughing but I've just taken a very large drink of coffee and I can't swallow for laughing. I'm laughing that hard that an involuntary fart exits my posterior, which creates even more laughter. I manage to compose myself just in time to swallow my coffee as it starts to dribble down my chin.

One particular day, I was going to work, and I asked my husband to wash both cars whilst I was out at work. When I got home I asked my husband about his day, had it been a good day, and did he manage to get both cars washed? He said that he had washed one of the cars.

I started to grumble at him and fired lots of questions at him. I asked why hadn't he washed both cars and what had he been doing all day. He replied, 'Think about it, Sam.' I paused, thought, yep, I had nothing. His words were: 'How can I wash both cars when you've gone to work in one of them?' Conversation finished.

One evening I took child 2 to a martial arts class.. We set off earlier than usual as I know one of the main roads we usually travel on is under maintenance, so I don't know which way to travel. After running through the different routes in my head, I finally pick one.

En-route I decide to telephone the husband as I know he will be driving home from work, and we can have a little talk. He asked where I was. I began to tell him the full story of my journey and explained it was taking longer than usual. I said to him, 'In three minutes I will have been on the road and driving for 30 minutes,' and he responded with 'so you've been travelling for 27 minutes then'. I went quiet for a minute while I worked it out and then laughed. Why didn't I think of that??

My parents were at my home for our lovely Easter Sunday family meal. I asked my family if they were enjoying the food. My mum made some noises of contentment and said she was thoroughly enjoying the vegetables. I said, 'Really, mum?' in a disapproving tone. 'How can someone like vegetables more than roast and mashed potatoes and slow cooked shoulder of lamb?' I replied, 'I don't eat that many vegetables.' Child 1 interjected and said, 'You have them every day for your tea.' I said, 'No, I don't eat vegetables, I eat salad for my tea.' There was a chorus of 'what do you think salad is?' to which I responded with 'salad isn't a vegetable!' then they all laughed and proceeded to mock me (all good, it was banter). I honestly didn't know what salad was, but I honestly didn't think it was a vegetable.

Misinterpretation

A source of amusement to me and for others.

On a recent trip to the lovely town of Chester, me and my husband were walking along the streets, full of shops and restaurants. I noticed a sign above a restaurant and said to my husband with much excitement, 'Oh look, a Greek restaurant', then I realised it said, 'Geek Retreat'. How the chuffing hell did I get Greek Restaurant from Geek Retreat??

Another time I came home from a shopping trip, and as usual I went into all the details of what I had been up to and the shops I had bought items from. I pointed at one of my purchases and said I bought this from the GAD GET shop (the shop's logo was circular; the GAD was in the upper half of the circle and the GET was in the bottom half of the circle). It wasn't until I was saying it out loud that I realised the shop was the GADGET shop.

One time my fantastic hubbie surprised me with a two night break away to celebrate our wedding anniversary. The hotel was lovely, quite modern and a little bit posh, not mega posh but posh enough. We checked in, unpacked our bags, and went for a little walk before heading back to the hotel. The bar area was extremely quiet, so we ordered drinks and sat down. I scanned the area, taking it all in. The staff were busy prepping for the upcoming evening meals, setting the tables, looking at the diaries. There was a small area of an open kitchen, and I watched the chef. He carried a paper sack and walked to what looked like a very large tabletop pizza oven with a fold down door. I looked at the sack and it appeared to be a very large paper bag the type you can bulk buy potatoes in from a farmer, he unravelled the top and poured some of the contents into the oven

I remarked to my hubbie, 'oooh look, they have oven baked potatoes, I bet they taste amazing'. As I continued to watch, the chef poured more into the oven. I thought to myself, 'they're weird looking potatoes, I've never seen black potatoes'. The contents of the bag were coal. Cue the WTAF look from my husband, followed by fits of laughter.

Oversharing

Good old oversharing; from what I've read it's quite a typical autistic thing to do, I wasn't aware of this until I received my diagnosis.

Do I still do it? – Oh yes, countless times and it can still be embarrassing.

For years I would just spill my whole life story to anyone I managed to interact with. The number of times I've had a gentle kick under the table, or a sly hand put on my back or leg to indicate that I'm waffling on to people about things that I really shouldn't be saying.

Pre-diagnosis, there have been multiple times when I've been told off for sharing too much information and giving out details to people I hardly knew. I honestly did not know what I had done wrong. I felt like I was innocently talking to people, engaging, and telling them about my life, I wasn't aware certain subjects were out of bounds. Turns out they are.

Turns out that my innocent oversharing was used (by certain individuals) against me, leaving me devastated and struggling to cope.

There are many times when I walk away from a chat, and I begin to question why I've just said what I've said. I ruminate about all the things I've said, sometimes shaking my head and grinning to myself in disbelief. Onlookers must think I'm mad.

I mean, I've noticed that I even overshare when returning a product for an exchange or refund. A simple, it doesn't fit or it's broken would suffice but not me – the poor staff member gets a chapter and verse of why I'm returning an item.

TRUST

I think that many NDs and NTs have issues with trust, and I find it especially hard. I've been lied to, let down and used. I was naïve and vulnerable, and I think being autistic made it easier for me to be let down.

It's been a tough ride to find friends and to be sociable, so when I found what I thought was a friendship I gave it my all, I gave my full trust, lots of my time and opened up, overshared. I wanted to be liked, I wanted to fit in. Sad as it sounds, I bought treats and gifts for people just so they would think more highly of me, like me more, I just got used and abused.

Now I'm older, with my diagnosis and being more aware of who I am, I'm more guarded. Don't get me wrong, I have still made the odd faux pas of being drawn in with people, but now, early on and with the help of my family I can start to see what they are really like, and once I see it, I start to distance myself to the point of little or no contact.

BELIEVEING OTHERS

Having my trust issues, is the reason I struggle to believe others. I think it's a consequence of past traumas, a time when I was vulnerable, having been let down and used by others. Or maybe it's also because people can be so full of shit.

On the flip side, if a person or persons don't believe what I'm telling them I can become very anxious. I become intensely focused and passionate about not being believed and must make sure that my words are being whole-heartedly accepted as the truth. I can repeat myself over again. I feel like a person in a witness box trying to get a jury to believe me. I need the person(s) to understand that I'm not lying and I'm someone who can be trusted and relied upon.

If I still feel the person(s) I'm speaking to doesn't welcome what I'm saying, I can get overly emotional and frustrated, which in turn can become anger or tears. Sometimes the outcome isn't how I'd like it to be and that is a challenge, it's a process that I struggle with. My own worst internal enemy comes into play – let the rumination and looping begin.

FRIENDSHIPS

My husband is my best friend.. The one I turn to for everything in my life, he's my confidant, my support, my rock, my everything.

Growing up I felt more comfortable being around males. I found it easier, they were less judgmental. I used to say that I was a bit of a tomboy, I certainly looked and acted like one.

People say that their children are their best friends, their mum or dad are their best friends, but my autistic brain sees these relationships differently.

My parents are there to guide me, to help me and be there, when needed.

I can't be my children's friend as I have a duty to parent them a bit like a manager. Being a parent means that my children are not going to like me at times for enforcing rules and routines. If I treat my children as friends, the parenting lines will become blurred.

It's a bit like an employer and an employee, I feel being friends/ friendly can cause problems in the workplace, you have a line that cannot be crossed.

Over the years I've struggled with friendships and I admire people who have a best friend or a group of best friends for many years. I'd see how they would go away on holiday together, go for meals and drinks, and how much they love each other. My heart would break a little knowing it's something I've never been able to have.

Overcomplicating Stuff

If there's a hard way to do something I instinctively find it. It's always the longest and hardest route that I take. Something can be simple, but I seemingly and naturally make it more difficult.

Why do I do it? I have no idea.

All I know is that what I'm doing makes sense to me and I'm unable to think of any other way of doing what I'm involved in. Whether it's working out a puzzle, using maths, doing DIY, or cleaning.

I can get frantically frustrated and upset if I can't work something out, but I don't give up, eventually I'll ask someone's advice if I feel like I'm failing. Then I realise I should have asked for help sooner.

'JUST GOOGLE IT'.

It's a phrase that we all use all too often.

I've used it too.

It's a great tool to have at my fingertips. Fact finding, looking at photos, diagnosing my illnesses, finding out where I have seen an actor before whilst watching a film or TV show.

BUT...

When I have an issue and I don't know how to solve it and someone says, 'Google it' instantly, it's panic on another level. It can send me into a frenzy.

If I can fathom what to write in the search engine I'm instantly hit with 'overload'.

Which answer do I pick? What website do I click onto first? Which is more reliable? It's lots of words and writing, which isn't great for me, it can be too overwhelming.

Organisation

I like to think that I have great organisation skills; however, the husband does not agree.

There's nothing better for me than having a plan, an itinerary of what's happening. I have to know what's happening day in and day out, in fact I have a need to know what all my family are doing each day. It doesn't have to be a detailed plan, just a general what they're doing.

What's my husband doing today? He's at work.

Child 1 – at university, that's ok

Child 2 – School, that's ok

It affects me when my family venture outside of the norm and don't let me know. If I know they are due to arrive home at a certain time and don't appear, I become very unsettled, it becomes unbearable for me, my emotions and brain activity go off the scale. Meltdowns have been known to occur.

CHILDREN

From birth, my children had routines, feeding times, bath times and bedtimes were a must. By doing something so natural to me had a positive outcome as it gave them a sense of security and stability. I never had any issues with my children refusing to go to bed or kicking off, it all worked beautifully.

There were rules with playing with toys and games. I'd struggle with the untidiness and disorder, and I couldn't wait for it to be tidy again. There were times that I insisted that my children had to put some toys away before they started to play with their other toys.

My children were always taught to use manners, to behave and to tidy up after themselves. I once had a standoff in someone's house. Child 1 was small and had been playing with their toys (they had a child of the same age) and we were leaving. I asked child 1 to put the toys back where they belonged, child 1 refused. The host' said, 'oh it's ok, I'll see to it'. I responded by no. It was a Mexican standoff with me and child 1, I told child 1 we weren't leaving until the toys were back where they should be. Eventually child 1 relented and we left. The other adult said, 'I wouldn't have been able to do that.'

I will say, all through the years my children have been growing up, I have had multiple amazing compliments on their behaviour and them as people. People would comment to my parents too when they took the children anywhere.

I struggled with my children bringing friends home; it has occasionally happened but I'm so happy when they left.

Child 1 is 19 and I think there has only ever been three sleepovers, child 2 hasn't had any. I simply can't cope with it. When any of their friends came, I simply couldn't relax, and I masked to a silly level, I'd just act way over the top, my voice changed, it was all so weird.

There were lots of times when one of the children came out of school and said can their friend come home with us and play (right there and then) and I'd make an excuse every time. I did say that we could arrange a play date if we pre-planned it.

I had a fear of my children going to visit their friend's houses too, I felt out of control and couldn't keep them safe. It also meant that I would have to pick them up from an unfamiliar street, an unfamiliar house and have to do that socialising stuff.

All situations such as these always made me question myself as a person and my parenting, I always felt 'not normal' for feeling and acting in this manner. This is a reason why I'm truly thankful for my diagnosis for making me realise I'm not a lunatic with horrific parenting skills, that in fact, I am autistic.

PLANNING

I plan everything, anything you can think of, occasionally I over-plan and overthink in way too many details. If my plans don't go to plan, I struggle, struggle to adapt. At first, panic, anxiety, fear, anger ensues, and I can't think straight, but eventually I calm down and accept the new changes.

I also tried to plan my family's lives too and it goes down like a shit sandwich.

My to-do lists are my everyday thing, they mean a lot. Lists help me crack on with life more comfortably and easily, I suppose it's the routine thing.

I write them on scrappy pieces of paper, notebooks, on my whiteboard, or I have a mental note of what I'm doing. The mental note can be chaotic as sometimes I forget something I needed to do and then I will hyper focus on what I haven't done until I manage to do it!

The lists I make for myself often cause me unneeded angst and pressure as I feel I must complete all the jobs. I carry on like a Duracell battery at times to the point of burnout or meltdown.

My hubbie is always saying I give myself too much to do and it all doesn't have to be done in one day. I can't make him understand that I can't leave things, if it's on my list to do that day, I really must do it. There have been occasions when I've failed my list of tasks and it causes me heap-loads of stress and then it loops in my brain until I've done it.

HOME

Everything in my home must have a place, a designated place. Clean, tidy, organised spaces for everything.

Furniture items need to be situated correctly, on lines, in line, nothing slanted or tilted. Blinds must be opened in a certain way; curtains aligned with even gaps at the top. Towels folded and put on the radiator with edges lined up together. Beds made in a certain way.

Cans in the cupboard turned around so the labels all face front and in line. Bathroom items arranged neatly and correctly and stood like soldiers.

Bottles of water lined up in a perfect order. Lined up equally, and we take from the set up in a particular order or so I'd like it to be. Unfortunately, in the house there are family members who take random bottles from anywhere in the line up and it does my head in.

Having a clean and organised home makes me feel very calm. Mess makes me anxious, sometimes to the point of meltdown. It appears quite absurd to the husband and child 2 when I have extreme reactions over what is seemingly something trivial. Such as the cooking tongs are put in a different section of the drawer divider, or a water spray bottle from the bathroom cupboard is on a shelf with bubble bath instead of with the hair gel and comb.

SUPERMARKET PACKING

Husband – He opens the carrier bags and puts anything and everything in the same bags.

Me – 'Oh my God, what is he doing', No, just no, stop it, please. 'Why would you put anything for the fridge in with the bathroom items?'

When I start to stress at him, he does laugh at me and then like a naughty child, he does it even more just to wind me up. Good job he rarely comes shopping.

Packing carrier bags must require organisation.

Chilled items in one bag.

Frozen foods in another bag.

Produce on its own.

Kitchen ambient products together.

Bathroom products in a separate bag.

Some items can share the same bag but only along the same lines, like chilled and frozen, or kitchen and bathroom ambient products.

In my brain, it makes unpacking and putting the shopping away much easier?

PACKING SUITCASES

It's a military process that starts with lists.

Lists within lists to list all that I need to pack. Once the list has been done, I can start to compartmentalise everything.

> Cosmetics for the face and hair – Face cleaner and pads, hair serum, hair gel, hairspray, razors, shave gel, hairbrushes/combs, water spray, hair accessories, Vaseline, tissues, toothbrushes, toothpaste.
>
> Cosmetics for the body – shower gel, deodorants, moisturisers, aftershaves, perfumes, hand cream, suncream, after sun.
>
> Medication – any tablets we may need, sudocream, plasters, germolene.
>
> Underwear – bras, pants, knickers, socks.
>
> Swimwear – shorts, bikinis, cover ups.
>
> Day wear – whatever I think we all need for lounging around or going on day trips.

Evening wear – Clothing suitable for evening meals, whether casual or formal.

Footwear – Flipflops, sandals, trainers.

Accessories – Sunglasses, hats, towels, contact lenses, glasses, phone chargers, pens, reading material, sweets for the journey.

Documents – Passports (if needed), insurance, medical cards, money, boarding passes (if needed).

I've never been able to understand how people can throw items into a bag or suitcase and just go.

For me it can be a lengthy process but it's how I operate, listing all items and marking them off as I go enables me to be relaxed as I know we have everything we need.

I am frequently laughed at for the number of items and suitcases I take away with me. I find it tricky to decide what to take with me and I have to ensure that I have all things needed for all eventualities.

16 days old at my first ever photo shoot.

Back at the photographers with my cute little dress.
Mum loved this dress so I had two, one in red and one in blue.

Mum rocking the 70s look while I zoned out in my dress with the blue elephants on. :)

The decor that triggered my first-ever sensory overload. What were my mum and dad thinking.

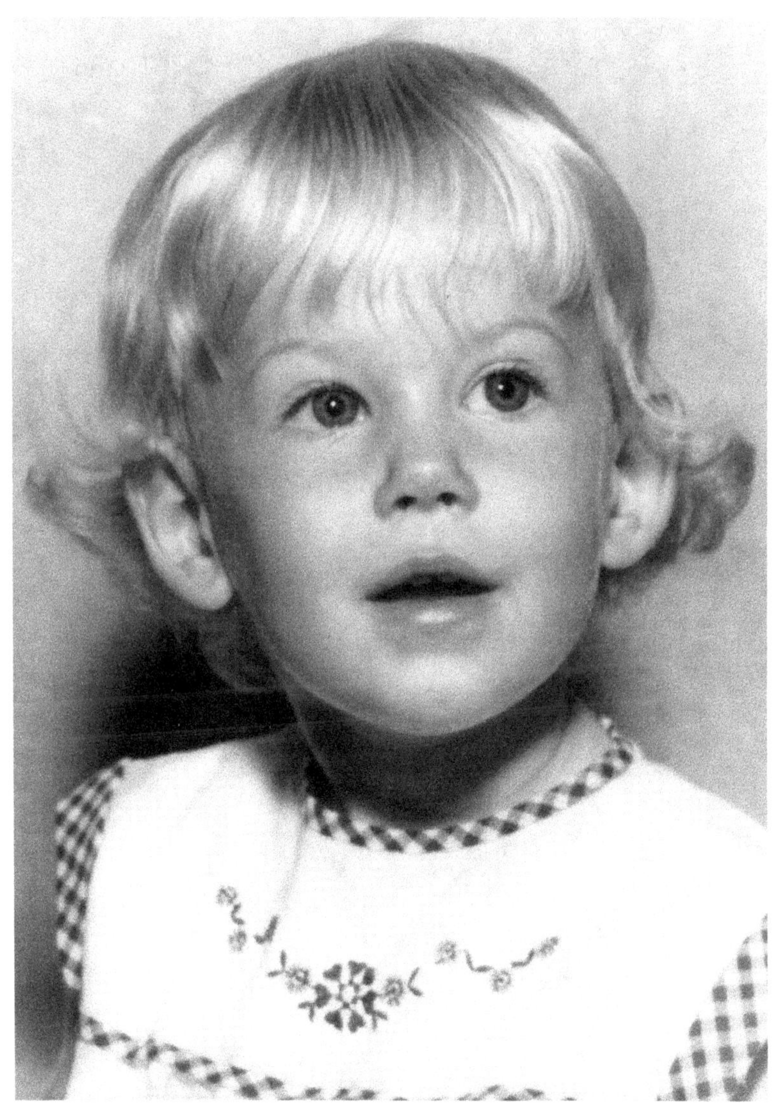

One of my mum's favourite photos of me.

A special family trip. Look at the hair and Dad just what were you thinking wearing those desert wellies and socks!

Meeting Worzel Gummidge and Aunt Sally.
A cup of tea and a slice of cake, anyone?

When life got a bit too much.

Such a cutie.

One of my favourite photos.

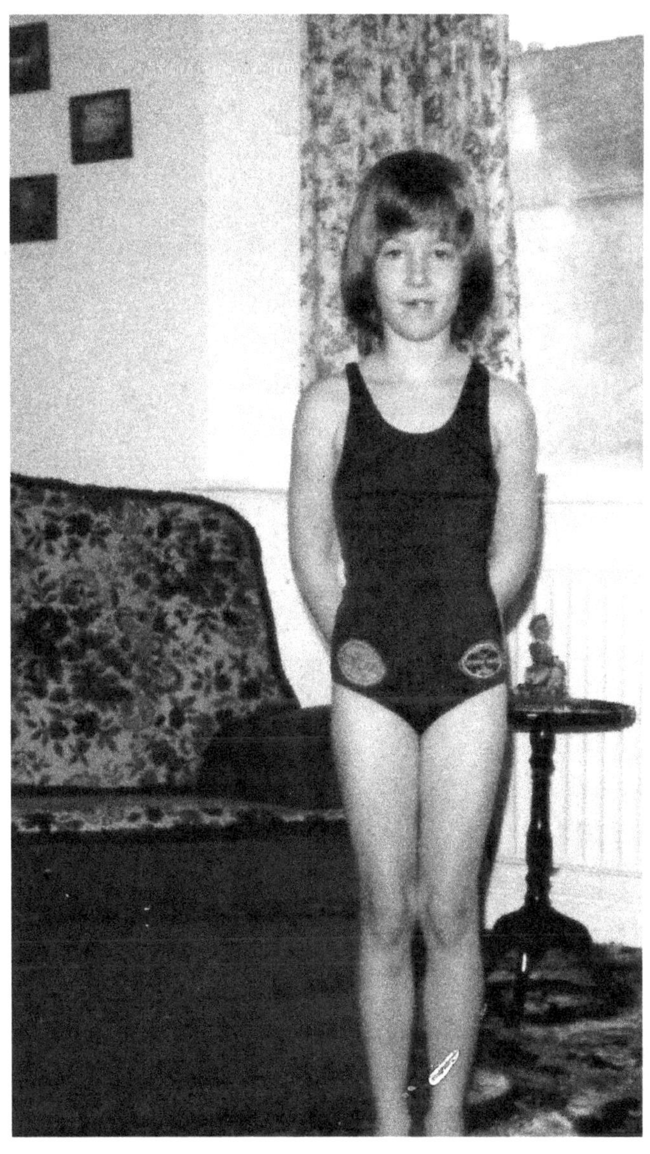

Good God, what even is this photo?

My last ever school photograph.

Camping at the El Delfin Verde in Spain.

My first ever, proper night out and I was ridiculously anxious.

Pretty blue eyes, beautiful blonde curls and a tan.

When I thought cutting my long, flowing curls off would look nice!

One of my favourite photos of me as an adult - so far.

Perfection

It's a 'big issue' (no not the magazine sold by people on the streets).

I hold myself to very high standards, everything must be done to a certain level, and to my standards.

I think the need for order and consistency plays a huge part in my 'perfectionism'. It brings order and regulation to my overwhelmed, meticulous, precise, and detailed focused brain.

Any imperfections are like a red rag to a bull, a flashing beacon if you like. My brain then holds the focus on the imperfection, and it sees the upset and becomes uneasy by the failures in inconsistency and quality.

At school I remember the teachers telling my parents that I'm good but can be slow and steady as my work must be perfect.

Everything must be done correctly, and I hate making mistakes. I fear getting things wrong.

To get things wrong feels like THE worst thing. My brain starts to overthink, how has it happened, and I MUST MAKE IT RIGHT.

To make sure I'm doing something correctly, I will ask every question I can think of to make sure I understand it before beginning, I can even question the answers to the questions I've already asked.

My husband can get annoyed at me for asking lots of questions when he feels that he has answered my queries satisfactorily.

SPOTS

I feel, come under the 'perfection' chapter.

I see spots as imperfections and have quite a spot-squeezing addiction. My kids have been on the receiving end of my addiction to squeeze, they're older now and are not as willing to let me poke their zits and blackheads. My husband doesn't mind me attacking his spots, he secretly likes spot popping.

Oh, how I love blackhead squeezing, I'm one of those gross people that love to watch spot-squeezing videos.

Now I'm older, I've learned that spots are not such a bad thing, but I still want to desperately pop them ALL.

I will never know how individuals can leave blackheads to develop, like for 20 years – WTAF!

Have you ever watched any YouTube videos of spot squeezing? Oh, my word, it's amazing, I love it, watching the videos were one of my hyper fixations at one point. =)

HAIR

My hair is naturally wavy, if allowed to dry naturally (after combing) it looks bloody awful, sort of a wiry, frizzy, dried-up mess, aka a Brillo pad, if you like.

If I wash and dry my hair in a certain way, it can look gorgeous. Once done, my hair has to be a certain standard for me to be happy. I've been known to have a meltdown if my hair won't style the way I need it and then it affects whatever else I'm planning to do.

I don't have my hair relaxed and down very much, as once it's been coiffured for a night the next day, I wake up looking like Don King, so it must be put back up in a ponytail.

I can only tolerate my hair down for a few hours too, as after that the hair touching my face and neck becomes annoying (in an unpleasant sensory way).

Putting my hair in any ponytail can be tricky too as I like the hair going into my ponytail to be smooth with no lumps and bumps. I will re-comb my hair into my pony tail as many times as needed to get it as close to smooth as possible.

DIY

I don't mind DIY; I'll have a go at many things but not electrics. DIY takes me quite a long time as I have to have things (you guessed) PERFECT.

Silicone lines have to be just right, which may mean I silicone, wipe, wipe too much off and must do it again and again and again and again. Cutting, fixing, sanding, all need to be on point. With painting I have ways in which I need it to be, so it's routine based, the lines need to be as straight as I can possibly get them.

I won't allow decorators to update my house as I know they won't do it in the way I do. I allow tradesmen to do jobs that I can't (which are many) but I'm a pain in the arse, I question everything. I ask them why they are doing what they are doing, what materials they are using and why. I scrutinise it all.

When the workmen have gone, I'm looking at all their work from that day and if I see anything that's imperfect or doesn't appear right, I

a. have to have Q&As with the hubbie about 'the thing' or
b. have my brain totally consumed with the issue until the tradesman arrives back at the house and then I can bombard them with my uncertainties.

What's cool now is that I can tell them about my autism and quirks and that's why I will ask loads of questions.

There's been times when things aren't right, and confrontations have to happen and it's SHIT. I don't like confrontation, yet I seem to be drawn to it. . I think that maybe the words I use, how I use them and possibly my tone of voice creates upset when I don't mean to.

It must feel like I'm CID-interrogating them.

The way I'm dressed, my hair, the cleaning in the house, DIY – like painting, applying silicone – it all must be on point. On point in the way my head thinks it should be. I've had meltdowns if I've been unable to create the 'PERFECTION' I crave. If it's not 'right' in my way, I do it again and again and again until it is.

CLEANING, WASHING, AND IRONING

Throughout the years I have had to have help from child 1 and the husband as there are things I'm unable to do. Oh, the stress, I don't want anyone else to do it but then I don't have any choice. All I see are imperfections, faults everywhere. Bits being missed, half-arsed cleaning. So, as my autistic mind goes into a tizzy, the words just flow out of my mouth as to what mistakes I see and then a bloody argument starts. Every chuffing time, no matter how I say it..

As child 1 and child 2 grow up, I am trying to make them more self-sufficient. I'm teaching them and encouraging them to be part of the daily duties such as cleaning and keeping of the house. You can imagine how grateful they are for this, can't you?

I don't want them to grow and leave home and they be unable to look after themselves. Child 2 is less enthralled to be led down this path..

I couldn't entertain a cleaner either for the same reasons.

Unless I'm well and truly physically unable and on my own, I wouldn't be able to employ a cleaner, it would be too stressful.

RANDOM STUFF

I have a little stool with a cushion that I sit on when doing my hair and make-up that sits very neatly under my little vanity desk. When the stool is placed away under the desk the edge of the seat and the legs line up perfectly with the edge of the desk. When my husband uses my stool to sit on whilst drying his hair he never, ever puts the stool back where it lives. It's always halfway out, on an angle. It drives me friggin crazy.

I can be getting undressed and noticing that the top of my bedroom curtains aren't how I need them to be. So, whilst half-naked with my bra half-on and half-off, I will walk over and straighten the curtains. The imperfection of the curtain is more important in that moment than finishing getting changed.

ADDICTION OR MY AUTISTIC ROUTINE?

I hated taking tablets when I was younger, can't say I'm a fan of them now either. My mum had to crush them up on a spoon and mix them with jam or anything sweet so I would take them.

In fact, I think that I ended up with a fear of trying to swallow pills.

Throughout the years and sometimes now I take a pill and the little shit gets stuck at the back of my mouth, at the start of my oesophagus and I go into panic mode. I end up looking like a dog or cat when they are retching.

Ever had paracetamol get stuck at the back of your throat and it starts to dissolve? It's rank, I'm shuddering right now at the thought of it.

Coated capsules seem to slide down the gullet much better than the uncoated ones, yay for this invention.

I've now mastered the art of taking tablets and supplements. I take a rather large mouthful of water (but not too much, it's got to be just right), then pop in the supplement or tablet, I wait until it's floating and then I go for it. Sometimes, the tablet seems to be in my mouth for ages trying to get it to float but I can't chance swallowing if it's not floating as I know it'll get stuck somewhere it shouldn't, and I will panic. Sometimes tilting my head back helps if I'm struggling.

There are a couple of supplements I take that are round and rough and the only way I can take these is with a drink that can make the tablets smoothly glide down the oesophagus, e.g., a protein drink, milk, or orange juice.

THE YEAR 1999

I suffered an injury that would change my view on medication.

Prior to this I saw any medication as a 'no-go'. I didn't want to put anything such as 'drugs' into my clean and healthy body.

The injury I sustained caused my severe pain and trauma that I needed ongoing help with. Scans, physio, Osteopaths, and tablets.

Around 2016 I was offered a new tablet to try and help with my ongoing pain issues, these were Co-Codamol tablets.

I'd never had anything like Co-Codamol before, within a few minutes of taking them I would get a 'buzzy' feeling. Morning pain has always been the worst so having two Co-Codamols as soon as I opened my eyes really took the edge off my pain.

If I can remember correctly, I started on a low(ish) dose then it was increased to 30/500mg. I was prescribed two to be taken up to four times per day, so 8 in total.

I quickly fell into a routine of taking two as soon as I got up and then I took another two as close to 11am as possible, another two at about 15:00 and then another two before bedtime.

I had medical reviews with doctors about my prescription and my Co-Codamols were on repeat.

A doctor at the pain clinic in the Hospital said he was more than happy for me to continue taking the Co-codamols since I was able to function day-to-day.. The doctor said people with this injury were reliant on wheelchairs, stuck on settees, don't really have a life and are drug dependent. I was more than happy and relieved with his words, so I continued to take upto eight co-codamols per day.

Fast forward to 2020, Covid.

Me and my better half had had our Covid injections, wore masks, stayed vigilant and followed advisory procedures. Child 1 tested positive for Covid-19, within two days the husband was positive and four days later I was also infected.

Child 1 wasn't too bad but boy it was bad for me and the husband; thankfully, we didn't need to go to hospital, but I did think at one point I would have to ring an ambulance for him.

After two weeks my symptoms were slowly disappearing, every day for the two weeks I had taken all the paracetamol, ibuprofen and Co-Codamols I could. As my recovery began, I decided that I'd had enough with the medication and I was going to stop taking it all, and that's what I did.

Eighteen months prior to this I had just stopped taking my anti-depressants, just stopped, not weaned off them and I didn't have any trouble. There were no side effects, nothing.

I assumed that it would be the same with the Co-Codamols – HOW WRONG WAS I?

Within days of stopping taking the tablet, I had all sorts of issues, but I naively thought (at first) that it was still the symptoms of Covid-19 until I read about what Co-Codamols are.

'Co-Codamols contain codeine, which is an opioid, which can cause addiction. You can get withdrawal symptoms if you suddenly stop taking it'. Erm, yep, didn't realise this.

Oh, dear God, I was withdrawing and didn't know what to do with myself. I had been on them for about six years, I thought about taking a few just to try and help, but I stood fast and went cold-turkey, I suffered but I got through it.

I genuinely did not think I was addicted to the tablets; they became part of my routine and as I like routine I took them at the same time, every day.

How was I medically allowed to carry on taking such a high dose for such a long time? Money, maybe? Did I slip through the net? I now wonder how many undiagnosed people are out in society who are addicted to substances due to the same reasons?

Prior to my diagnosis I had been on anti-depressants a couple of times and to be honest they didn't really do much. Post diagnosis I realise that it wasn't anti-depressants I needed, just a diagnosis to help me understand me, my brain, and my thoughts.

Sensory

SMELL I have a heightened sense of smell.

I'm a bit like a blood hound or sniffer dog. Comically, I can stand somewhere with my nose twitching, focused and not moving. Just like the Grand high witch sniffing for children in the Roald Dahl's classic, 'The Witches'.

It's quite cool to have my heightened sense of smell but sometimes I really wish it was toned down a tad. Child 1 always comes to me with something to smell. Mum does my top smell? thrusting the armpit section under my nose.

Obviously, the smells out in the countryside or the sweat of others I'd rather not be able to smell as keenly as I do. Especially the rather pungent ones like stale BO that is so bad that it actually smells of onions!

I've had a few experiences on a treadmill at the gym where the person next to me is breathing quite heavily and their breath comes my way. Once the smell hits the inside of my nostrils, I start to Hyper focus on it, it's all I can think about. It eventually starts to make me feel sick, so I'll try and breathe through my mouth with no inhalation. It gets a bit tricky when I try and drink my water though. I also make sure I don't breathe heavily just in case my breath smells. I just pray they will get off the treadmill quickly, so I don't have to suffer for long.

HEARING

My hearing is another of my heightened senses. The noises that people make seem to be amplified, like people chewing, sniffing up, breathing. If someone eats a bag of crisps and the room is silent, I can't cope, the constant crinkling of the bag when someone's hand is going in and out, the sound is unbearable. I start to feel a build up inside and I want to bark at them, shout at them or take the crisps off them so I can make it stop. But I don't. I just walk away until they've enjoyed their snack.

With my sensory stimuli in full swing my startle response is heightened too. I'm a very jumpy person, very easily startled, which can be comedic to some level.

There's nothing funnier than watching a person's reaction when there's a loud bang. I admit, I laugh, and I laugh at myself sometimes, other times not so much.

I seem to scare at anything being dropped, doors slamming. It's almost as if I'm constantly on edge.

I've had times when I'm startled to such an extreme that it makes me angry, I can't control my emotions and then go into meltdown.

My brain has been unable to deal with the sudden onset of the noise or touch.

VOLUME

'Why are you shouting?' a question that makes me stop for a few seconds while my brain lets the words sink in and then brings to my attention how loud I am.

I recently apologised to my physio when I had a sudden realisation that I was talking way too loudly. I think the whole department heard my conversation.

I'm so frigging loud at times and I don't realise.

When there's a family get together and by that, I mean my parents, me, the hubbie and kids, it's stupidly loud. My parents can be equally as loud as me. It's like the noise levels in a pub. It's loud, then it gets louder and louder and dulls somewhat and then starts again. I'm sure people on the next streets can hear us.

I've noticed that my voice and my speaking tone alters dramatically when I'm talking passionately, when I've been trying to prove my point, or I think someone disbelieves what I'm saying. Is it that subconsciously I think that my noise levels will help me be taken more seriously or by having more passion that people are more likely to believe me?

When I'm elevated a usual sarcastic comment from my husband is, 'Why is your voice so high? Dogs can hear you', 'You better check the glass in the house as I think you may have smashed some of it '.

With my hearing being one of my heightened senses, I can find loud noises a bit overbearing, and I am quick to point out when my family are talking too loudly. Yet, I talk loudly; doesn't make sense, does it?

I believe that it's a common trait for autistic people to be louder than normal and to not realise. There can be lack of control, some of us may speak too loudly, others too softly. The speed and tone of our voices can be tricky to regulate too.

For an autistic person talking normally can require a lot of purposive effort.

TOUCH

Soft cuddly toys were a 'thing' for me for many years of my life, I loved them, but I only liked ones with a certain fabric. I've now swapped cuddly toys for dressing gowns, lol.

Back in the day when I was small my mum used terry towelling nappies and she would cover my nappies with 'rubber pants'. I developed a thing with these 'rubber pants/cover ups' or whatever they were. I loved the feel and would constantly rub them between my fingers and if there was another child wearing them, I'd want to feel their 'rubber pants' too. Most children have a blanket or some sort of material square they like the sensation of. Me, it was rubber pants.

From a very young age until today I have a 'thing' with stickers, Sellotape, or anything with that sort of tackiness. Once the tackiness has reduced, I dispose of whatever I have in my hand and get some more (if there is any). There are stickers that have a different feel to them, I have to test the sticker before I make a decision whether I like it or not.

If any item has a sticker on it, I'm drawn to it and pick and peel to see if I can get it off, shower gels, body butters, the square white ones that are stuck on the insoles of brand-new trainers...?

The calendars I buy have stickers to help markup special events and dates – not in my house, the stickers are for my fingers to play with.

It's quite frustrating if the stickers don't come off easily and rip. My family (in jest) say they'll just buy me a roll of Sellotape for my birthday and Christmas.

Back in the day, when I was little the supermarkets that my mum would shop in had individually priced items, priced up by a pricing gun. When you reached the tills, the employee would key in the prices on the till.

That was how it should have been. I decided to make this more challenging for all involved. I would sit on the seat in the trolley and take the stickers off all the grocery items with the prices on. I'd have them stuck all over me but mostly on my skin. It wasn't so great for my mum or the cashier when it was time to pay, and nobody had a clue how much anything was, and a frantic time was had trying to get the prices for the items.

I've lost count of how many times I've jumped out of my skin and made a loud shriek or squeal when I think there's something crawling on me, and it turns out to be a strand of sodding hair!! If it does turn out to be something alive and crawling on me, that's me done, I'm flapping around like a chicken, looking a bit hysterical.

I hate the sounds of flies, bees and wasps close to my ears too, it always startles me.

I'm not sure why but when I jump or act like a chicken, I always laugh about it. I wonder if it's a nervous laugh or a laugh of embarrassment.

I'm not great with some types of substances on my hands, yet I'm happy with others. For example, when I'm cracking my breakfast eggs and I get some of the white on my hands I wash them straight away, it's a foreign object on my hands and I've got to get it off. It happens multiple times until I've finished with the uncooked eggs.

I can't stand my wet head hairs stuck on my hands or in between my fingers – ARRRGGGHHH. The process of washing my hair is a challenge anyway but having to stop and remove hairs on my hands frequently makes it a long process.

I can, however, use hand cream and it doesn't bother me. I can cope with any glue that gets on my hands as I can pick it off and it gives me satisfaction. I mean who as a child didn't lather their hands at school in the PVA glue just so they could peel it off?

Maybe, picking the glue off gives me the same feeling that I get from picking my skin.

As I sit writing this paragraph, we are having some beautiful, sunny, and hot weather and I love it, yet it does create some issues for me, going to the gym and exercising is one of them. Not attending the gym is not an option and I've got a goal to achieve so whatever the weather I'm there. But in weather in the high 20s it's not pleasant. The feel of the sweat that starts to run from the top of my head downwards is ridiculously uncomfortable, it's a horrible feeling and it plays havoc with my senses. I can't imagine what I look like to others, wafting my two pink face cloths about, wiping my body every time I sense a bead of sweat exiting my body.

Recently on our sunny holiday we had some extremely hot days with very little wind. I was trying my best to relax and even tried to take a snooze on the sunbeds, but it was impossible. My body was sweating so much that it felt like I had insects crawling all over me constantly, it was horrid.

Wet clothing against my skin is an awful feeling too, not just wet from my own sweat but if it rains and my clothes get wet, the feeling is indescribable, I just have to get changed as quickly as possible. Have you ever worn socks and stood on anything that's wet? I usually use a few choice swear words and take off my socks, dry my foot or feet and then go get another dry pair.

Don't get me started on what it feels like having socks and shoes on and my feet getting wet, especially when I have no access to change them.

I get a strange sensation too when my skin gets wet and the water dries naturally, the area becomes really itchy, and it drives me bonkers. Yet, if I get out of a bath or shower and get dried with a towel, my skin doesn't feel itchy – weird, I know!

I also know when my period is going to arrive as I sweat through the night while in bed and it's gross. The feeling of the damp material of the bedding and covers – eeeeewwww.

Ever since mother nature blessed me with the monthly occurrence of the red river, it's been tough in a sensory way. From the off I've never been able to use tampons but it's not for the want of trying. As a teenager and starting your period was a huge deal and I remember at school having 'the talk' about periods and the products that can be used. The talk was mostly about using Tampons. The ones with applicators and then the ones without where you get to use your finger to shove it up. WTF, I was mortified and couldn't believe people actually used them.

I bought the ones with the applicators. I was anxious beyond belief, and it took me quite a while to try one, my shaking hands didn't help. I stood up all proud that I had done it, but I could feel it inside me. I had read and been told that you shouldn't be able to feel the tampon once it's inserted so I started to fidget. Then I pulled it out and started again, then repeated, I had all sorts of thoughts going off in my brain. Eventually, I had to use sanitary pads, and this wasn't great either, all the rustling of the paper as I walked, and I was convinced everyone could see it through my clothes.

In my teenage years, I just wanted to be like the other girls, the cool girls,and periods was another thing that made me feel different. I actually thought that there was something wrong with me and felt dirtier than them because I had to use sanitary towels. Psychologically I felt less mature than them and not as cool because I had to use the 'older women's' products. It's mad to think that those were my feelings over sanitary towels.

Over my 30 years of needing feminine products, I didn't give up on tampons, every now and then I would give them a try, but the outcome was the same, I can always feel it so out it comes. As I've aged, I've realised not to worry about it anymore and stick to what works the best for me.

My husband has always wondered how women can bleed for up to seven days and yet not die!

A little story of sanitary towels.

One afternoon, whilst at home with both child 1 and child 2 (when they were young), I was preparing the family tea. I noticed that I couldn't hear child 2. I started to look around the house. When I opened the bathroom door, child 2 was sat on the floor next to the shower cubicle surrounded by paper. Stuck on the shower doors were lots of 'aeroplanes', child 2 had unwrapped lots of my sanitary pads and placed them on the glass doors, having a great time with the 'aeroplanes'.

I have a problem with having my blood taken and I've recently realised that it's the feeling of the needle in my arm that causes anxiety and stress including the build up to having my bloods taken. It's an object in my body that shouldn't be there and that cause me sensory discomfort.

I've come to the conclusion that I don't like something on or in my body that shouldn't be there, if I can feel it.

I'm quite happy to wear my eight earrings all the time as I can't feel them, but at night, I have to take the top pair out before bed. The reason being is the piercing position, when I place my head on to my pillow the back of the earrings twist and my ear doesn't lie normally and I can feel it. I tried to sleep with them in but after much tossing, turning, and fidgeting I knew I had to take them out.

VISUAL

I'd call myself hyper vigilant and have strong awareness around me. I'm forever spotting changes, sometimes it can be the smallest of things. I see them in people, on TV, in films, my surroundings, whilst shopping, when people have changed their cars, clothing, material items. In conversations I will say to my family did you see this or that and the answer is usually a 'NO'.

Buying cars/ material objects can be very time consuming and overwhelming as they all need to fit my requirements and sensory needs.

Put simply, I can't just make do with anything.

Suddenly running out of my everyday items or someone eating the food I've specifically bought for myself can send me into panic, it's like the world's going to end. If, on my shopping day the supermarket doesn't have my items or foods it causes chaos in my brain. I need to make sure over the next few days I can locate what I need from anywhere to have a sense of fulfilment and calmness. I can't rest until I have everything in my home or possession that I should have. I like to make sure I have plenty of multiple items, like, lol – everything.

CO-ORDINATION

What's that?

I don't have any, lol oh and I'm clumsy.

I'm forever bumping into stationary items, banging my head, tripping over, getting bruises.

Guess what, it's something most autistic people have to deal with too, who would have known!!

In my adulthood I tried taking part in fitness classes, but they didn't last long, I hated them, I was too close to people. I also felt stupid when I couldn't keep up with the class, they moved left, and I moved to the right. The others would raise their hands and I would be doing God knows what with mine.

COLOURS

I find pastel colours very calming, in fact most of my house is decorated in what I would call calming colours. I find bright and intense colours and lots of patterns very harsh and disturbing so it's better that I stay with pastel.

STIMMING (SELF-STIMULATION)

I think I'm quite subtle with my stimming, even my family struggled to identify any.

I pick around my fingers, I pick the skin around my toes, I pick my toenails, I pick the skin on my feet. I also scratch and pick my psoriasis on my scalp. It's all a bit yuk really.

My hubbie says I tap my feet.

My hand movements are quite frantic at times, I gesticulate lots almost as if I'm shouting with my hands.

When I'm agitated my head movements become more pronounced, I open my eyes wider, emphasising my words. Almost like I'm glaring.

I'm a bit of a fidget arse too.

Food

Aaarrrrrggggghhhhhh (no other word for it is there really?).

I think it's fair to say that many folks with autism have a difficult time with food.

How painful is it? The weirdness, the pickiness, the textures, and the bits that we can't really explain.

Loving eating the same safe foods but then after a while you can't eat that food ever again as the sight and smell of it makes you feel sick.

My issues with food started when I was very young, I wouldn't eat much at all, and when I did eat it used to take me an eternity to finish it. I don't think I did finish many meals.

My mum, through panic and desperation, used to try and force feed me, and I wouldn't have it. I'd just sit with my mouth shut and my lips locked tight.

I was waif like. My mum panicked so much about my reluctancy to eat that she took me to the doctors. The doctor's response was that I would eat when I was hungry and to just to give me what I would enjoy.

Fish fingers and chips were a staple, even into adulthood. I love a fish finger sandwich, now with hot baked beans and occasionally cheese. The cheese melts with the hot food and gets all gooey. It must be white bread with butter, the butter has to go all the way to the edge of the bread, where it meets the crust and four fish fingers, which fill the bread area very nicely. The crust is controversial – if the crust is soft then I can eat it, if there's any stiffness, the crust will not go anywhere near my mouth.

In my childhood years in order to eat like a Sunday dinner this process had to occur.

I placed the mashed potatoes on to my plate and patted them down flat into a circle shape. On top of the potatoes were mashed up carrots, patted down in the same way and then I would spread apple sauce on top of the carrots. I would then make a hole in the middle and that's where the gravy and meat would go.

Sometimes I would just eat the mashed potatoes pressed down in a circle with apple sauce spread over the top.

I ate lots of biscuits. Bourbon creams were my ultimate favourite, and I loved the proper Jammie Dodgers. I would hold one in my hand and nibble around the biscuit in a circular motion until all the biscuit was gone. I would then be left with the circle of jam in between my thumb and forefinger, I'd give it a squeeze then place it in my mouth and let it melt until it fully dissolved.

I obsessed over Coco Pops until they changed the milk brown and then I couldn't eat them. I LOVED Rice Krispies, Weetabix, and Sugar Puffs. I can still eat big bowls full of Rice Krispies, the milk cannot be higher than the Rice Krispies but just enough for me to pat them down and be submerged underneath the milk. Got to eat them quick though before they go soggy. Weetabix continued to be a staple breakfast for me until a few years back

– but I stopped eating them as 30 minutes after, I was hungry again. I concluded that there must be better foods to eat.

My battle with food continued over the years. I always had my safe foods and wouldn't deviate at all. The thought of trying anything else just freaked me out way too much. After meeting and marrying my other half, I became a little more adventurous with food. I do wonder if it's because he makes me feel safe and I trust him.

With new food and drinks there's always a process to go through.

First, I ask loads of questions about what it is, then I make a weird face and stare at it. Then comes the obligatory sniffer dog test. At which point my husband blurts out, 'Get it eaten!' Next comes the lizard tongue and the tentative touch of whatever it is on the tip of my tongue before I shudder with the taste or respond with, 'it's not that bad or it's ok'. At times, I kind of know, on first impressions, whether I'm going to struggle with a new food and no amount of coaxing is going to get me to eat it.

Gagging at the texture and taste is another distressing part of eating. I've found it happens more when I'm eating some hot food and it's gone tepid or cold, the colder it gets the harder it is for me to put it in my mouth. Swallowing is even harder. It gets to a point when I stop and can't physically eat anymore. If I find, let's say a hair in my food or a bone in the fish when I'm eating something, my whole mouth has to be emptied. I'm then in a quandary whether to carry on eating. I'm gagging just writing this.

'You'll eat it if you're hungry' erm, nope I can't. Looks like I'm going to starve then.

Child 1 trying a new drink: 'Would you like to try it, Mum?'

'No, but I'll smell it.' I sniff if for a few seconds then put the glass to my mouth and manage to wet my tongue to see what it's like.

Child 1: 'Oh, you sniff with your mouth, do you?'

We both laugh hard.

Honestly, I could write a full book on the foods and drinks that I dislike, or the ways in which I must prepare them to be ready for consumption.

I thought of sharing a few examples of my daily food trauma – it's both quite amusing and traumatic at the same time.

MINT

Child 1 was quizzing me on my food dislikes and asked, 'Do you like mint?'

I replied, 'God NO' – 'but you eat mint jelly with dinners, and you like after eights and chewing gum', but I don't like mojitos they taste of mint.

I can't stand Mojitos, but I will only drink Chocolate mint Whey Protein powder. I will eat mint sweets and mint chewing gum but once the crunchy bits of the chewing gum have dissolved (or whatever they do) I'm ready to get the chewing gum out of my mouth. If the chewing gum stays in longer and it becomes 'gummy', 'rubbery', I can start to retch. I like mint jelly but not mint sauce, there's just something about mint sauce that a bit yuk. I'm not keen on mint choc chip ice cream but I love mint chocolate, especially the new Terry's chocolate orange that is Mint?

BANANAS

'Would you like a banana milkshake?' – 'don't like it, it tastes of banana' – 'but you like bananas' – 'yes but I don't like things that taste of banana'. I'm not a fan of them when they have any green on them, if they are a bit green, they leave a weird coating on my teeth and it's YUK. I can't stand them when they are getting too ripe and the dots cover the yellow skin, at this point they are mushy and there's the stringy bits when you peel them. Absolute reason to start gagging.

APPLES

Only the small, crispiest apples will do. I can't eat sour ones or any that have gone mushy. The ones I like are few and far between that I just don't buy them anymore.

PEARS

What even is the texture of a pear? No thank you.

FORTY TWO

TOMATOES

Another devil food, eeeeew. Why does every salad and pre-packed sandwich have to contain tomatoes??? Even when you pull them off the sandwich, there's always some sodding little seed hiding somewhere and the whole sandwich tastes of tomatoes. Many times, I've been unable to carry on eating it. Why did I pick the sandwich with these ingredients on, you may wonder. It's the best out of a bad bunch or what's left, rather than starve I had to choose something. And why is all ham and bacon smoked? Another thing that gets on my nerves.

We once stayed in Wales, near to the Mach Loop. I've stayed in better accommodation; it needed updating and I had the worst sleep. Morning came and I was looking forward to the breakfast, it was set out lovely with lots of choice. After cereal, I ordered a full English but taking ingredients off and asking for it to my liking. By the time it arrived, I was hungry, and it looked so delicious, so I started tucking in. As I cut a piece of the amazing bacon and lifted it, my facial expression changed, I smelt it. Bastard smoked Bacon, I was fuming. It wasn't listed as smoked on the menu, why is it assumed everyone likes smoked bacon and why can't menus be more specific? Streaky Bacon is a BIG FAT NO too, unless it's pigs in blankets and the bacon is that well done that it crunches when bitten.

Back to Tomatoes =)

I can tolerate the tinned ones in a Spaghetti Bolognese or tomato sauces if I ever have a lasagne. I'm ok with the puree tomatoes on a pizza but not too much or I have to scrape it off. I find Dominos Pizzas seem to overdo the sauce or puree and it's a bit too much for my liking.

PORRIDGE

I remember staying over at my nan's home when I was little and eating porridge. My nan had a way of making delicious porridge, I've never tasted any porridge like it since. My nan had two Tupperware bowls with lids on, an orange one and a yellow one, my porridge was served in which colour I chose and then I would sprinkle sugar all around the top before adding milk – Yummy.

Porridge as an adult.

What the actual fuck are those hard things in it??? The skin things that are ruining my porridge every chuffing morning.

They are just like those thousands of hard bits that you get in popcorn, I can't stand them in my mouth. I spend more time picking them out than I do eating the popcorn.

Every spoonful of porridge is checked and if I get too many hard bits, I start to retch.

One morning a conversation took place between me and the hubbie about the porridge I was eating regarding the hard bits. I asked him what they are and showed my disapproval of them being in my bowl.

My husband laughed at my description and in a sarcastic manner pretends to be me in a restaurant: 'Excuse me please but could I order some porridge, and can you make sure that it has no hard skins mixed in?'

I still don't know the correct name for those yucky things.

FAT ON MEAT

I'm like a surgeon, meticulously cutting it all away to make sure none of it gets in my mouth. If I buy any meat sandwich, I open it up and spend (what feels like hours) picking at it to make sure it's ok to eat. If it's a hot sandwich, by the time I've done picking and pulling all the fat off it it's a cold sandwich and then it's highly likely that I won't eat it.

I think I have an issue with fat on meat after an incident whilst I was at Junior school (many years ago). I was sat eating a bacon sandwich, I remember taking a bite, chewing it, and swallowing. The next thing I know I was in blind panic. I had some bacon in my mouth and some down my throat attached together with fat that, I felt like I was choking. I couldn't get it out, I couldn't separate the two bits of bacon either. I don't know what happened next, but it put me off eating bacon for a long time; when I started eating it again, I had to have it cooked really well done. To this day I still like well-done bacon.

I can't eat sausages anymore due to the texture and the little lumps of fat that you get in them, once I get a grisly blob of fat, it puts me off eating it. It's the same with mince, there's always little fatty lumps in that too.

CHICKEN

I have to say it's one of my favourite meats to eat but it's not without issues. The body transformation I'm undertaking means I eat a lot of chicken. I'm allowed to eat certain fish but as I don't like it, I'll stick to chicken. After trial and error, I've got my routine with my chicken perfect for me. I buy full chicken fillets in large packs and then separate them and bag them ready for the freezer. I don't handle them with my hands though, that's just nasty. Then I start to dissect them. I use a fork and a large pair of scissors to cut each chicken fillet. I snip off any remaining skin, and clumps of fat, I remove any bits of blood and skin in the middle of the fillet, then I cut into chunks ready to freeze.

If the older generation saw what I cut off the chicken fillets and what I throw away, they'd be raging. I can just hear, 'what you are throwing that away for, wasting money, I could make something with that'. All I know is that what I'm throwing away saves me from retching if I get any in my mouth after it's been cooked.

Once I'm ready for a new bag of chicken, I take it out of the freezer and defrost it. Then as I take it out of the food bag, I cut it into the tiniest pieces (even smaller than bite size) into a dish. The smaller the better as it cooks quicker but it's so much easier to eat.

I do like chicken thighs as they are super tasty, but they contain fatty lumps and pieces; if I get this fat in my mouth then gagging may ensue. Chicken thighs then become annoying as I spend precious eating time pulling them apart to find and cut out every miniscule of fat within, and then of course they start to get cold which adds to the difficulty of eating and swallowing the meat.

Mini chicken fillets are ok but in the middle of each one there's a strip of skin that if I get it into my mouth makes me retch, so these have to be dissected too.

Chicken drumsticks are not really my thing unless there's no other option. How do people put the whole thing into their mouth and chew it and suck the bone as they pull it out? Yep, you guessed it, I have to dissect them before eating it or else it's a gag fest.

Another issue I have with chicken is smell, if there's a slight or unusual smell with uncooked chicken (or any meat for that matter) I will throw it away.

I recently revisited a local butcher's shop adjoining its factory. I thought with the amount of chicken and meat we eat in the house that it may be cheaper and better quality than buying it with my weekly shop from our local supermarket. In my first visit I loaded up my basket and bought quite a bit, which included two trays of 2kg chicken breast fillets + 200g free.

Once I got home, I opened the first tray ready to separate and dissect them for freezing. My nostrils were hit with a 'funky' smell. My initial reaction was, 'always happens to me, I've bought a pack that's going off'. I opened the other tray and it smelt the same, I didn't think that they both could be off and thought it was maybe my sense of smell was a bit too sensitive. I carried on with the job of mutilating the chicken fillets. I usually leave a couple out of the freezer, which last me a day before having to defrost another bag.

I ate some that same day, and I was ok, so I convinced myself I was being overly sensitive to the smell. However, the next day as I opened the freezer bag, the smell was stronger, and I threw the chicken away. The same happened with another bag that I defrosted, so I threw that away too. I returned all of it back to the shop and the customer service was great, it was all sorted. I got some replacement chicken, bought some more items, and went home. Unfortunately, every single time when I have bought chicken from them and opened it, I got the same smell, so I have stopped buying from there. I mean they sell large quantities of all their meats including chicken, but that certain smell just turns my stomach, and I can't deal with it.

I'm back to buying my supermarket fresh chicken fillets each week that luckily have no smell whatsoever when I cut open the plastic.

STEAK

Call me fancy if you will but fillet steak is the only steak I can truly eat without any problems. The reason for this, is the lack of fat on or in a fillet steak. Yet all the top chefs and my husband always say you need fat running through the steak to give it a better taste. My answer to that is, 'No thank you' and here's what happens.

I begin to eat the steak and as I chew, I can't break it apart in my mouth with my teeth or tongue, so I start to use my fingers to try and pull it apart whilst it's in my mouth. Generally, I become grossed out with it, can't cope, and end up with a mountain of half-chewed bits of steak with attached bits of fat piled up on the edge of my plate. It must be as close to the edge of the plate as possible so as not to touch any of my remaining food.

All our family love steak.

There are generally leftovers that get refrigerated but I can't eat it, even when it's been reheated or soaked in gravy the next day, I just can't consume it. The texture changes and so does the taste.

FISH

I love fish from the Fish shop or chippy as I like to call it, but I'd never order fish in a restaurant. I've tried many times to have fish at home, but the smell and bones are extremely offputting. I see other people tuck into fish and sit there pulling out loads of bones and by the time they get to eat it it's cold too.

I seriously don't know how people eat all that other seafood and shellfish stuff, like cockles, muscles, welks, prawns, crabs, etc, to me it's grim. There's no way any of it is going near my mouth.

YOGHURTS

I can't eat yoghurt with fruit bits in them but I can eat yoghurts with chocolate balls or chocolate bits or even biscuits in them, but not fruit pieces. It's got to be smooth.

JAM

Only jam with no bits will do.

EGGS

When I crack them open, I remove any cloudy white lumps and stringy bits and anything that's attached to the yolk before I can move on to cooking them. Fried eggs must have a runny yolk but no snotty bits in the egg white WHATSOEVER! If I get snotty bits, I gag. Ordering these in an eatery, can you imagine. 'Excuse me but can I please have fried eggs that are runny but not snotty'? and then they have to try and cook them just to my liking.

I'm happy to report that I'm no longer a poached egg virgin. I can honestly say that the look of them being cooked and served on a plate was enough to turn my stomach. However, on a recent trip my husband ordered some for breakfast and I ordered the same. He was as shocked as me with my choice. I have to say they were cooked very well and tasted nice too.

Would I have them again? – Yes, but not often as I think they would make me gag.

CHEESE

I've always loved cheese but only certain types. It was always Red Leicester and Dairylea triangles; any other cheese was a no, no.

I have become more adventurous and like lots of different cheeses now, especially brie, but I draw the line with that blue cheese stuff. I also think that I have an intolerance to extra mature cheese. When I eat it, immediately the area just under my eyes start to sweat, sounds hilarious. Can you remember Aunt Sally from Worzel Gummidge (if not you may have to look it up)? She had the two red circles on her cheeks. That's where my cheeks sweat after eating extra mature cheese.

FYI - I met Aunt Sally and Worzel Gummidge when I was a child.

Eating out in restaurants and pubs is a hard thing to do, no doubt many of you readers will know exactly where I'm coming from. I have safe places to eat but even that can be tricky.

Through my teenage years and into my 20s (probably all of my 20s) my go-to meal was a starter of garlic bread, with a main meal of Gammon, eggs, pineapple, peas and chips, then followed by chocolate fudge cake.

We hadn't eaten out for a while and we decided to visit one of my safe places, 'Pizza Express'. I know what the food is like, I know how it comes, I know some members of staff, so all is good.

Until...

We arrive, sit down, and read the menu.

PANIC STATIONS.

The menu had changed, and my usual food wasn't on the new menu. I couldn't concentrate on the menu, anxiety kicked in and I didn't know what to do. I ended up having a mini meltdown and started to cry.

My husband said we could go somewhere else if I wanted but that would have been equally dire.

After I calmed down, I spoke to the waiter about the menu change. I explained what I usually had, and he told me that I could alter one of the new menu items to get it to my liking. I was so relieved and then went into my usual, 'well I feel stupid now' mode. I then overexplain myself to my family why I acted the way I did when, really, I shouldn't and don't have to explain myself.

I will say that Pizza Express are great at helping me with my food. My usual is one of their salads, but I take five things off the original and add four things that I like and it's never a problem. It's always yummy.

Another problem I have with eating out is I don't know what ingredients the food is cooked with, like herbs, spices, and oils. I genuinely think that I am sensitive to spices. My husband jokes and says, 'anything spicier than chicken soup is too spicy for you'.

I've had countless food disasters after ordering an item off the menu which theoretically I should be able to eat from the description on the menu.

I don't like pepper (as in salt and pepper), it makes me feel sick and it's way too spicy (go on and laugh, my family does). Loads and loads of places cook with pepper, why doesn't it say so on the menu?

We once dined at a gorgeous little Italian whilst away on holiday in the UK, it was an unfamiliar place for me, and it takes me ages to pick my food. I question everything and then go for something that I should like and that is like a food I've had before. I ordered chicken, potatoes and vegetables, the chicken was in a sauce that I've eaten many times before and I was really looking forward to it. Child 2 ordered his usual pizza and my hubbie chose a beef tagliatelle dish. The food came and it looked and smelt delicious, we all tucked in. But after a couple of mouthfuls, I looked up at my hubbie and he knew by the look on my face something was wrong – it was lathered in cracked black pepper, I nearly cried, I couldn't eat it. I did try a few more mouthfuls but I just couldn't do it. My mouth was burning, and I felt sick. My hubbie tried my meal and thought it was amazing, I tried his meal and that wasn't great for me either. I agreed to try child 2's pizza to see if I could eat that but NOPE there were some herbs on that pizza that made it unpalatable too. I sat there and got a bit drunk and had a bag of crisps on the way back to the hotel.

I'm not allergic to foods but I have so many sensitivities or maybe dislikes that makes eating foods incredibly tough.

I would like to see cooking ingredients used implemented on the menus in eateries, but I don't think it will happen.

I don't like spicy stuff either and so many restaurants use spices in cooking. There was a time I visited a fast-food place to have a chicken wrap. It's an eatery that you go along the line and pick what ingredients you would like on your wrap.

I went along the counter choosing my food.

I picked, what looked like, boiled onions and mushrooms. I say, 'only a few please', too many mushrooms make me gag and I will leave my food. I chose plain chicken, a few spinach leaves, grated cheese, and this time I chose what looked like homemade coleslaw. Coleslaw is another food that sometimes I can tolerate and other times I can't stand. My wrap was finished off with a quick squirt of garlic mayo.

It looked lovely, my mouth was salivating. I tucked in, oh my word it was gorgeous UNTIL...

Something in the wrap started my mouth and tongue tingling, I kept eating but the burning got worse. WTF is causing this, why is it so spicy?

WHY, just WHY. I couldn't see it being the onions and mushrooms, so it had to be the coleslaw but has coleslaw ever been spicy?

That was it, meal over, I was hugely disappointed and still hungry.

I have since used the eatery, but I haven't had the coleslaw again and it's been ok.

I would love to be able to eat anything and everything. I'd love to be able to visit any place and not have to spend ages looking at the menu trying to find something that I may or may not be able to eat.

I would be so happy if I could just eat any foods that no matter how it looks or what the texture feels like, I could consume and enjoy. But it won't happen, I am made this way.

Food recap – I don't like most things that are stringy, lumpy, watery, too well done, crispy, that taste too strong, foods that smell funny, look odd and I'm sensitive to spices too, lol.

Drinks

I'm a water baby and I don't mean I like being in it, well I do like my baths. I love to drink water but not tap water; it must be bottled. I hear people say all bottled water is the same or it's just tap water bottled up. I can assure all those nay-sayers that there is a difference and it's not all the same. I have to drink it mostly at room temperature. I can't drink water straight from the fridge or freezer, but I can drink a glass of water with ice, and I can drink cold water when I'm in a hot climate. Yep, it's all sorts of weird.

I'm not a fan of dilute juices or fizzy drinks but I love an orange Fanta when on holiday, there's something different about the taste. The downside is they give me gas.

TEA

Would you like a drink?

- Yes please, can I have a cup of tea? A baby tea please?

Baby Tea?

- Erm, yes please, I like it to taste like tea, but I like lots and lots of milk.

COFFEE

I've become more used to coffee as I've aged. I'm now able to have nearly half a teaspoon of coffee granules, whereas when I started, I could only manage a few coffee granules on the very tip of the spoon – any more than that and I couldn't drink it as it was too strong. People always laughed and said why did I even bother. I can't drink coffee anywhere other than my house unless they use Coffee Mate and it must be the real deal, the authentic brand. I cannot, not for the want of trying, drink coffee with milk. Just another quirky thing I do!

ALCOHOL

It's a love-hate relationship.

IN MY YOUNGER YEARS.

I was visiting my nan (the same nan who made the yummy porridge) and I remember being in her house and I told her I felt sick so she asked if I would like a cup of tea? Off she went and came back with one of her special cups filled with tea; I remember that it smelt funny. I was very much cajoled into taking a drink, my nan's power of persuasion must have been good, or I was too scared to argue!

I followed her instructions to drink it as it would make me feel better, but I instantly ran to the toilet and vomited. My nan wasn't lying – it made me get rid of my sick feeling by throwing up.

It wasn't until I was much older that I knew what the smell was in the cup of tea she made for me – it had a sneaky shot of whisky in it. To this day I cannot abide the smell of whisky.

My relationship with alcohol has been, well, strained at times.

I've never been much of an alcohol fan, purely through not liking the taste of most alcoholic drinks but as I got older it served a different purpose for me.

When I went on holiday with my parents and a friend, I was allowed to buy a little drink from the supermarket and I always chose fizzy rosé wine; I could stomach one or two drinks, no more. I remember one time I had a bottle of my dad's small bottles of beer, it was warm, I opened it, drank it and not long after I threw up. I've never been able to drink beer since.

There were the times of being out with my secondary school friends and it was the 'thing' to get 'pissed' on a Friday night in the park. I always felt uneasy, a bit awkward but I wanted to fit in, and I wanted to have friends and be liked, so I joined in. The drinks of choice were Mad dog 20/20, Castaways and White Lightning. Fuck my life, 20/20 was bloody awful but I managed with certain flavours.

In my later teenage years, I did like Taboo, but it was more like pop. If I couldn't get Taboo, I'd be upset and knew I couldn't drink anything else.

I couldn't understand why I wasn't like anyone else and why I wasn't keen on alcohol; it played on my mind, I just wanted to be like others.

I had a few years where I became more relaxed about not liking alcohol, accepted it. I think it was because I had a different focus in life. I had become engaged at 18 years old. Married at 24 and became a mother at 25. But by the age of 26 I was going through hell.

When my ex-husband left, I found alcohol again. It started when I came across the mini bottles of wines that my place of work had just started to sell. My thoughts were that they are small and inexpensive which meant if I didn't like it, I hadn't wasted much.

The night I took them home I remember sitting on my living room floor, my back propped up against my settee, I was on my own, the house was quiet, and I was sat sobbing. I opened the wine bottle and was pleasantly surprised by the taste. I was shocked that I hadn't tried red wine before. Instantly, I started to feel a bit more relaxed, followed by the feeling of being 'merry' and I liked it. The effects it had on me happened quicker due to the lack of food I was eating, the lack of sleep and my world falling apart.

I carried on buying the small bottles and then I began buying the big ones. Luckily, I didn't become addicted but my relationship with alcohol changed from this point in my life.

I've had times when it became a routine of mine, it got to the point where I didn't enjoy it or necessarily like it, but I would do it every night, it would start at the same time, and I would make sure there was always alcohol to be drunk.

I've had some really bad times with alcohol too, I'm one that seems to get drunk quickly on not much alcohol. I've landed myself in what could have been very dangerous and life changing situations too. One night, I went out with a work colleague, we weren't close colleagues and I still wonder why we went out together. That night, I drank before going out to our local town, I was pretty much drunk on arrival, I had more drinks and then the night was a blur. I found out that we had gone to a kebab shop and multiple men had tried to get me into their cars, none of which I could remember. Thankfully, my colleague helped me, and I got home safe.

I would, and sometimes still do, have a drink of some sort whilst getting ready before I go out for a meal or to a gathering. That first drink enables me to feel relaxed, it helps me to cope with what I will be facing, it helps me not to feel like a coiled spring when entering new places, it helps with the social aspect when I feel so uncomfortable. The problem is that I need that feeling to continue and having more alcohol is the only way to keep the feeling. I love the new confidence it gives me, the confidence that I don't feel without the poison in my body. Maybe this is why I get drunk quite quickly but then it all goes downhill.

I don't like the feeling of being really drunk, it's awful. I don't like being sick, it's a bit of a fear of mine, being sick comes with excessive alcohol drinking and it happens. If I drink to excess, I get anxiety attacks through the night. I would always wake up around the same time, 02:00, with my heart pounding. My brain would be racing, I would be panicking trying to remember anything and everything from the previous night. The next day I wouldn't want to look at my phone for what I may or may not have done. In fact, often it's been a great night, but I still panic. I'm not one to laugh and shake it off, it would severely and negatively affect me. Alcohol is a depressant though.

FYI – Vodka is not my friend.

Once time has passed, I am able to see my alcoholic antics in a better light and laugh about them.

When people say, if you don't like how it affects you, then don't drink. For me it's not that easy, it makes my feelings and emotions easier to deal with.

I wonder how many undiagnosed female autistics have issues with alcohol or are alcoholics?

Clothing and Accessories

A pain in the arse area of my life.

Apparently when I was young, I always used to take my clothes off, hated them against my skin.

As an adult I have always disliked shopping for clothes, trying to find things that fit and that I think look and feel ok is just the hardest thing ever.

In the past I have bought clothing because I thought it looked nice or due to the fact, I couldn't find anything else and then I instantly regret my purchases. I try to convince myself that I do like what I've bought and that I will wear them; however, the clothes and shoes just sit for years in my wardrobes until I gain strength to send them to the charity shop.

Now I'm older and a bit wiser, I like to think that I make better decisions, sometimes, at least.

There's a testing process that I have in place now for when I want to buy any new clothes, it's called the 'Itchy, scratchy test'.

Firstly, I feel the item with my hand, if the item passes that process, I then rub it against my face to see what the material is like on a different part of my body..

Imagine having eaten a meal and it's got quite messy and you're wiping your face with kitchen roll or a napkin, that's what I look like when doing the 'itchy, scratchy test'.

I must look like a right plonker to anyone who's seen me do it.

Soft and squidgy feeling clothes are my thing, no wool or cashmere. I don't get Cashmere, it's expensive and supposedly is all this and that, not to me it's not, it's itchy and scratchy.

What is it with the tags or labels in clothes? Do the people making the clothes have a training course or go to a special school on how to attach the most irritating material known to man? I cut them out of almost everything that I own which is great until I want to order or buy another of the same item, and I don't know what size I bought and can't find the item number too.

The joys of finding an item, that is good on a sensory level, looks good on me and I'm happy with, can give me so much satisfaction. I can get extremely giddy. I get that excited that I buy lots of the same item but in different colours and wear them over and over. It was always a puzzle why I did this until I read it in a book about autism and it's kind of an autistic 'thing' to do. Knowing that it's quite a normal thing in an ND world made me feel, well more normal.

Here's a few of the things that I buy/have bought in large quantities.

Converse High top footwear.

Nike Air Jordan's Retro 13 (only have two pairs as the UK don't sell them very often, otherwise I'd have a few).

Black sport leggings from Asda, I haven't found any that's as nice.

Ipanema flip flops (the best). I've got nine pairs at the minute and if I could, I would wear them all the time. I wear them at home when renovating much to my husband's disapproval. Years ago, we had some external building work done on our garage, and whilst there was muck and mess, I decided to rip the back of our home apart at the same. My husband told me we would do it after all the external building works, but the hyperfocus and obsession kicked in and I didn't listen. I knocked internal walls down, moved doorways, ripped off all skirting, architrave, and coving. I ripped out our en-suite shower room which meant taking off all tiles, taking out the toilet, sink, shower, everything. I single handedly removed all the rubbish too and I did it all wearing my FLIP FLOPS. My husband looks at what I'm wearing in a disapproving manner and always makes a sarcastic comment, something along the lines of, 'see you're taking health and safety seriously today'!

Sports vests from Nike.

Superdry hoodies (I love these SOOOOOOOOO much). I like to wait until the sales after Christmas and I get them loads cheaper which means I can buy more. Normally between four and six but they last me a full year.

Earrings, sterling silver (as other metals make my ears go manky), sparkly, shiny ones with all different colours of gems in them.

Cross body bags (I haven't got many now as I realise, I don't need them). I just feel safe with them, they sit on my hip so nobody can go rifling through my bag like they can with other handbags.

Character rucksacks (when I was younger and before children). Oh my, I loved these I had about seven or eight and they all had their own individual coat hooks. I can't remember them all, but I had 'animal' from the Muppets, 'fozzy bear' and a 'groovy chic' one. I'm still partial to a rucksack but only for the gym and going on holiday.

SOCKS

Socks just serve a purpose and that's to put a barrier between your feet and the shoes you need to wear outside. Nothing more, nothing less. There are only certain socks I will buy to wear. I don't dislike socks but as soon as I get my shoes off, the socks are off too.

I see people wearing socks all misshapen and twisted, how do they cope? Can they not feel the misalignment?

I've always got cold feet and the husband always says, 'why don't you put some socks on?' Erm, no thanks, I'll stick to having cold feet. What child 1 finds strange is that I wear slippers (slip on ones, with open backs) yet don't like socks on.

The reason is that the slippers aren't strangling my feet like the socks do, they're roomy inside. I love my slippers – they have to fit my sensory needs though and there are only specific ones that I can wear.

COMFIES AND NIGHTWEAR

I can only wear dressing gowns with a particular texture and feel.

Night dresses are a no-go, you wake up and they're wrapped around your head.

Pyjamas – the bottom of the PJs ride up your legs, the top strangles you and they twist around your body. It's a 'no' from me.

GOLDILOCKS CLOTHING – Not too tight, not too loose but just right.

Items of clothing can't be too close to my neck. Scarfs can't be too tight. The necks of jumpers have to sit just below my neckline. I love V-necks as nothing's touching my neck.

If my clothes are too tight, I feel like I'm suffocating, unless the item is stretchy.

All the seams of my clothing must sit against my skin where it's supposed to fit. Twisted seams drive me CRAZY, I can't bear it.

The long sleeves of any tops must be fully pulled down before any coat or jacket is worn.

If a picture could describe uncomfortable, this would be it.

HEELS

I've tried, I have really tried to the point of crippling agony. Me and heels just don't do well together. Add into the mix that I have quite a 'manly' walk and what you get is something comical. I look like Whoopi Goldberg in a scene from the film Ghost. Whoopi Goldberg is all dressed up and hands over a $4 million dollar check to the nuns, when she walks away from the nuns in her heels that is kind of like what I look like. Haven't seen it, please have a look, it's on YouTube.

How do women go to work in heels? How do they go on shopping trips in high heels? My feet can hurt if I go out in flip flops!

I've always wanted to look trendy and fashionable, cool and modern, when in fact most of my life I've looked like a bag of shit. Most of my life has been spent in sportswear and trainers.

On the other hand, when I do get dressed up and do my hair and make-up, people are often shocked to see me looking that way. Their reactions always make me smile.

BREAKING NEWS

I have recently discovered a new shop, new to me, it's probably been around for years. It's one of my new favourite shops.

'Hollister'

OMG! they have some incredible clothes that are super, super soft and squidgy, perfect for our sensory needs, especially in the boys/men's section.

Bedtime and Sleep

There's nothing I love more than getting into bed, with my sensory sufficient bedding, the mattress that's just right for me and the pillows I've finally found that are comfy.

The TV's on.

I like to watch a bit of TV at night before I go to sleep (or try to, I think you know what's coming).

Lights out time – LET THE FUN COMMENCE!! (Or not as the case may be.)

It all starts with what my husband calls the 'My Tribal War Dance' aka me trying to get comfy.

I push, pull, flick, tuck, untuck, move, manoeuvre the quilt into the exact and precise position.

The quilt must be high up around the back of my neck especially if my husband's face is facing the back of my head. It drives me crazy if I can feel any of his breath on my skin.

The quilt is tucked around me so there's no air gaps, apart from some of my face. Tucked evenly though so I can't feel any harsh lumps against my body. The only air I allow around my body is the air that comes from my backside when I emit gas from my anus..

My knees and ankles cannot rub against each other, oh god no.

My hair must be positioned on the pillows out of the way, I can't sleep in bobbles or anything else. I make sure I can't feel my hair on my face or trapped around my neck.

The pillow must be just so, not too lumpy on any side, front or back but balanced out nicely.

Feck my life pillows!

Another Goldilocks and the three Bears situation – buying pillows.

Not too hard, not too soft, the pillow must be just right.

My husband says I could have shares in a pillow factory with the amount I buy. When I go pillow shopping, it's quite a lengthy process as choosing the right ones is a hard task. There's been many times when I think I've bought the right ones and I come to use them and they're awful and I have to go and buy some more. I once bought some, 'forever full' pillows and to start with they were nice but within a couple of weeks they were changing and going flat. I complained to the company as they pillows are not as advertised, got a refund and had to buy some more.

To this day I'm still finding it challenging buying pillows. I can't stick to the same ones as the companies change the manufacturing process or discontinue my previous ones.

Sleeping in hotels is a nightmare anyway but trying to sleep on their PILLOWS – GEEZ. The number of times I ask for more pillows or check all the pillows in the room to see which ones I can sleep on. I have often taken my own pillows to hotels, which can make all the difference to the quality of sleep I have.

Now let the sleep commence, lol.

When the nights are good and I'm feeling quite relaxed, happy, or extremely intoxicated, I will drop off to sleep quickly.

Other times it's like my brain activation switch has been pressed. My mind starts to think about all the things I'm worried or stressed about and then it's like a free for all in there. My thoughts become majorly random and all over the place. Internally I'm shouting, 'WILL YOU JUST GIVE ME A BREAK?'

I'm all comfy now and ready to sleep...BUT AM I?

My ear's not comfy on the pillow, my arm's aching, my neck feels funny, I need to turn over. I try to fight it off but the urge to turnover gets bigger and bigger. The niggles I'm feeling grow and grow until I've got to move and the whole settling down to sleep process begins again.

What is it with needing a wee when you're all snug and warm?

Going to the toilet is the last thing I do before my bedtime dancing ritual. I then get all relaxed and my belly doesn't feel right.

My brain activity fires up and a hyper fixation starts. 'You need a wee', 'No I don't, I've just had one', 'Yes you do, you need a wee, your bladder is telling you', 'No I don't, I'm not going for one'.

I'm overpowered by the thoughts that I need another wee. I annoyingly drag my warm and comfy body out the bed and go back to the bloody toilet, and hope that once I get back in bed I can get back to how I was before..

Another weird ass thing my brain does through the night is singing.

I can start to stir in my sleep and a line from a song will play on repeat, over and over and over. I don't get anything more than the one sodding line and it will repeat over and over.

The song will be a random song of no relevance to what I've been doing that day or even that week, it's not even a song that I've been listening to, it's JUST there.

A recent one was,

'Tie me Kangaroo down sport' – WTAF! Who wants that playing out in your head at 02:00?

I can't even tell you the last time I heard that song.

It feels like an eternity until it stops playing in my head. Sometimes, if I'm lucky I drop back off to sleep again, other times my brain activity switch is pressed again and then it's anyone's guess when I can get back to sleep.

My sleep is rubbish to be honest – according to my Fitbit I have multiple times during the night when I'm awake.

I did have trouble with the deep sleep stage and I'm aware that it's an important stage.

DEEP SLEEP or slow wave sleep (SWS).

This is the phase of sleep that we are least likely to wake up from. It typically happens within an hour of dropping off to sleep, your heart rate slows down and your muscles relax. It's generally hard to wake a person up that is in deep sleep and if they are woken, generally the person will feel mentally foggy and possibly groggy.

Deep sleep offers physical and mental benefits. During this phase our bodies release growth hormone and work on building and repairing muscles, bones and tissue and immune system functioning. It can also regulate glucose metabolism and is important for cognitive function and memory.

Due to my lack of sleep and sleep disturbances I asked the doctors if they could refer me to an autism sleep specialist. I wondered if being autistic may be a reason for my sleep problems and would have loved to speak to a professional about it. After my previous issues with medication I didn't really want to take anything else.

I'll let you guess the answer that I got from the GP.

I'm now on a low dose of Amitriptyline, it has helped somewhat with getting more deep sleep but if my brain decides on high activity on a particular night the tablets don't do jack shit.

I don't know how accurate the readings are on a Fitbit

I do know, however that I never, ever feel refreshed and always feel tired.

Other things that aid my sleep are complete silence and darkness, the darker the better.

It sounds bad but I can get super annoyed at my husband at bedtime.

He lies down on the bed and I can count 1,2 and by the number 3 he's off in the land of nod, I prop myself up and look at him and I'm like, Jesus, fucking Christ! how is that even possible. I've said to him on one or more occasions, 'can you just not fall asleep so fast and let me fall asleep first, so I don't have to hear your heavy breathing or snoring while I'm trying to fall asleep'! His response is, 'you're just jealous' or he starts laughing.

Many autistic people have trouble sleeping for a variety of reasons.

But did you know?

One of the reasons could be including irregular melatonin levels.

I didn't.

Music, Films and TV

MUSIC

I love music, I love the way it can make me feel. It has a way of moving my soul.

Music brings out my goosebumps, makes me feel happy, I can cry as I listen to certain lyrics, certain songs can tigger past thoughts or feelings.

It becomes a form of therapy, drives me more into my own world.

Music can make my feet and body start to move in strange ways like I'm having some sort of spasm, much to the delight or disgust of my children who wonder what the hell I'm doing.

I was elated to know it's an Autistic trait to play a song repetitively and every time it starts over, it's like the first time you've heard it. It's nice to know that I'm not a freak by doing this, that's it's not abnormal or peculiar. IT'S TOTALLY NORMAL (for an autistic person) – Fucking YaY!!

I don't play songs on a loop whilst in company, I think I would be perceived as being completely mental or they would just want to throw the device out of the nearest window or door. Hence, why I repeat songs while alone in my house, car or through my headphones.

Repetitive playing can also have an adverse effect. If I listen to a song that much, I sometimes cannot abide listening to it again. If I never hear it played again for the next five-ten years, that would be perfectly fine by me.

I do find that the sound of silence can be a beautiful thing too. It happens rarely and when it does (and if I'm in a particular frame of mind) it can be pure bliss.

SAXOPHONE

Oh, the beautiful sound of the sax. My favourite instrument of all time. It's a bit cheesy but the sound of a sax gets deep into my soul and gives me incredible feelings, always has and always will.

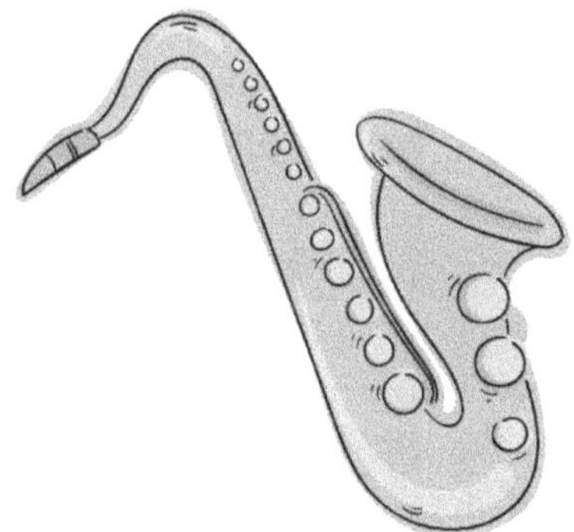

One Christmas about ten years ago my husband surprised me with an alto saxophone. I hadn't asked for it, I hadn't mentioned it, I opened it and cried. I couldn't play it but to have one of my own was just the best feeling ever. He had also bought me some lessons, but unfortunately, I had quite a long drive for my lessons, and they were held in someone's home. It was all a bit too much, so after the block lessons finished, my sax laid dormant for many years. That was until last year. I decided to find an online teacher and started to play again, and I LOVE IT. I'm not too shabby at playing either. My ability to learn is very different from most and I find it both frustrating and rewarding at the same time.

I'm so proud of myself for being able to do this.

FILMS AND TV SHOWS

Another interesting fact that I found out about autism was the desire to repetitively watch films, TV shows, social media videos.

I never realised I did this until recently, I noticed it more with child 1.

My go-to TV show that I used to watch all the time was 'Friends', it almost felt a tad obsessive.

Growing up my film was 'Grease', I enjoyed 'Grease 2', but it wasn't the same. If you imagine your childhood teddy bear that you love and someone buys you the same one, the second never has the same feeling as the first one. That's how I felt about 'Grease2'.

One of my adulthood favourite films is 'Pretty Woman' – at one point I had 3 DVDs. Another film I love is the Heat with Sandra Bullock and Melissa McCarthy.

With them all I memorised and recited the songs, the lines, and quotes from them all. I'd say them out loud in time, much to the annoyance of anyone who happened to be with me or around me. I'd do it with my music too, I'd rewind the music over and over so I could memorise the words. Weirdly, to me it felt like I had the ability to do something nobody else could do.

RBF

(AKA RESTING BITCH FACE).

Definition – a person, usually a girl, who naturally looks mean when her face is expressionless, without meaning to.

I'm told I have an RBF, a stern looking face. I also get called Scary, unapproachable and I once had a charming fella say that I have an RFF (or Resting Fuck Face). After seeing some recent images and videos of me I will admit it does look like I want to kill people.

I find that with my RBF it creates a barrier and it's sometimes tricky for anyone to approach me. I also know from experience that people easily form an inaccurate opinion of me. For those that don't pre-judge me and talk to me, they see something very different. Once the barrier of communication has been broken down and a conversation begins, they get to see the rather lovely me.

I used to get quite upset upon hearing this about me and I would deny it and feel slightly embarrassed and offended.

I totally own it now; and I know the reason behind it.

'I silently observe, I silently process and assess everyone and everything around me with uncertainty. I do this even in familiar places. I do this to see if there's anything new or any different people. I scan all the areas like I work for MI5'.

It's not only the RBF that's on show, but my body language changes. I can appear tense, twitchy, a bit spiky and look uncomfortable too. This normally resides when I've completed my assessments and I become more relaxed and settled.

Staring

It's safe to say, I stare, and I stare a lot, very intensely at times, almost glaring, with a side helping of frowning.

Often the words, 'Mum, you're staring' brings me out of it.

There are times when I don't know I'm doing it, I'll be looking at someone and it's not until they look at me that I realise I'm doing it. Sometimes, I don't mean to, other times I know I'm staring, I don't have a clue why, but I feel transfixed. I can be looking in someone's direction, but I can zone out.

Child 1 frequently asks me what I'm looking at and why, or what I'm thinking when I'm holding an intense glaze. More often than not, I'm just away with the fairies.

I tend to watch the behaviours of others, but I end up staring which can be deemed as uncomfortable to whoever I'm glaring at. I often observe, watching with intrigue, and bewildered by people's actions and body language and what they say.

I'm always doing it, yet I feel so uncomfortable when I'm being looked at. I can quite easily catastrophise when it happens to me. It can also trigger an emotional imbalance and meltdown.

EYE CONTACT

How uncomfortable is it?

I'll do it because I have to.

I'll do it to show you that I'm focused and interested by what you're saying to me.

Until...

I start looking at your eyebrows, your eyelashes, your nose including whether you've got nose hairs hanging or any bogeys (that will inevitably make me retch) or any snot dripping. I'll be drawn to your mouth, whether you're spitting whilst you talk, whether you have got white dried spit in the corners of your mouth (that makes me gag). I'll look all over your face, are there any spots and then I'll wander off looking at your hair, your hairstyle, all the other fine details that my autistic brain picks up on. By this point I probably missed some of what you are saying.

Here's another agonising eye contact moment.

There's a person coming towards me, do I look at them? Do I just stare at the floor? Do I look at that tree on my right and pretend that I'm doing some conversation work? Do I bend down and pretend to tie my shoelace? Do I walk right past them as if they are not there?

Do I? Make eye contact? But when do I make eye contact? How far away do I start to stare at them?

Do I look at them at the very last minute and see what they do first?

Oh, dear God, I'm locking in my stare, but I look like I'm possessed, and my stare might make them feel uneasy?

Do I make eye contact and smile? Smiling might make things feel less awkward unless, like me, smiling can be as awkward as eye contact!

Oh, dear God, I'm locking in my stare, glaring at the oncoming person, but I look like I'm possessed, and my stare might make them feel uneasy? But I feel I need them to look at me so I can smile or say hello, as that's a normal thing to do, isn't it?

Yep, a simple natural process is not so easy in an autistic world.

Farting

***Just call me 'GASSIUS CLAY' cos
my farts are knockout!***

Definition: To emit wind from the anus (this made me chuckle).

Farts or farting otherwise known as flatulence, botty burps, wind, gas, methane, mustard gas, shitting oneself.

It is indeed FACTUAL that autistic people are more likely to suffer with gastrointestinal problems. I'm happy to know this, it eases my mind knowing there's a reason behind my extreme farting.

My farts are often accompanied by my 'Muttley' laugh. From this laugh my family know that I've let out a botty burp – that's if they didn't hear it first.

I'm not one to shy away from talking about farting or letting one rip, in what child 1 calls 'inappropriate places' like taxis.

Or much to child 1's dismay when I ask one of the consultant doctors why I fart so much and why do they make all these different noises.

I've never understood how people get embarrassed by a natural human bodily function.

I've known people who say they have never dropped their guts in front of their partners – ever!

I've known people go to the toilet to fart – if that was me, I'd have to live in a bathroom.

I've known people be offended by the word fart and they stop people talking about it. WTF – get a life.

As a family we have so much fun with farting, I've laughed so hard at times a little wee has escaped but that's a story for another day.

I fart like a builder! – I'm a one-woman phenomenon with the sounds I can make.

- A mating Whale call.
- Air brakes being released off a truck.
- A motorbike.
- A Ferrari passing by.
- A trumpet (he plays the imaginary instrument).
- A door creaking.
- Floorboards creaking.
- A fly.
- A chair being dragged across the floor.
- Duck.
- Clap.
- Trombone.
- Tugboat.

According to my beloved husband the sounds in the list above are noises that my butt makes when I emit gas from my anus (there are more but I can't think of them).

I've had excessive wind all my life, sometimes it's been trapped wind that's caused me to be doubled over in pain to the point I thought I needed medical attention.

It's been like Doctor Dolittle played by Eddie Murphy when the doctor is called to give medical attention to a rat they think is dying. Whilst working on the rat, the rat farts and is cured, much to everyone's relief.

Money

Here it is, short and sweet, I'm shit with it (insert photos).

To be fair in the past I haven't always been shit. When I'm good, I'm good, when I'm out of control, it's been, well, tough.

If something is on my mind like renovating or decorating, I can become easily hyper fixated with things very quickly and it doesn't leave my mind until I can achieve it, fix it, or buy it. It has been dangerous.

Credit cards have not been my friend, I've made some bad decisions and some unfavourable choices, and I've struggled to deal with the aftermath. It's led to me having some serious meltdowns and continuous panic that can last for months.

The demons are real, I've felt like a spendaholic, a failure, an obsessive lunatic.

I make sure all bills are always paid and on time. I make sure that I have a list of all outgoings and set up direct debits for everything. I make sure I have a routine in place otherwise I can't cope.

I can be a tad fixated too when money is owed back to me, whether it be a person or a company. Until I have the money back in my possession, it will loop in my brain. If it's not returned as and when it should be, I will talk about it over and over until it's given back.

I have a 'thing' too that when I'm counting money, all the notes have to be facing the same way and coins must be lined up in size order.

Post-diagnosis, and I suppose, maybe due to getting older, things are much, much better.

Gifts, Presents and Surprises

Here's a good one. My face always says what I'm feeling. I once read a meme:

'I don't need a mood ring. I have a face' this is so me.

Surprises are such a lovely thing, so thoughtful, so kind, unless you are me – I have a serious dislike for surprises.

The fear of the surprise strikes me like a lightning bolt.

As a child, I loved Christmas but the thought of not knowing what was in the presents made me nauseous. I devised a cunning plan to stop me feeling yucky. While my parents were out, I would search for my presents. Once I found them, I would use a pair of scissors or a knife and slide along the Sellotape until I opened one end of the wrapped gift. I had a look at what I had then I carefully placed the wrapping paper back into position and stuck it back down. When Christmas Day arrived, I was still giddy and anxious about all my presents, even though I knew what I was getting.

Receiving presents and having to open them in front of people is tough, even with my own family. I can be seen as ungrateful when receiving gifts, but I don't mean to be. I'm just not a person who can pretend to like something.

As time has moved on my family now ask me what to buy me to make sure I'm happy and content. I get upset if I've asked for something and don't get it or it's not quite the same as what I'm expecting.

I'm not at all shallow or ungrateful, but each specific item I have asked for will mean something to me. It may be the texture, the colours, the smell; whereas if anything is bought for me that is different my specific needs may not be met. It could be a gift that will push me out of my comfort zone, like a gift to the theatre. My initial reaction may not be great, but when I've gotten over the initial panic it's the most amazing gift ever.

I do love giving surprises and gifts. I get lots of enjoyment from watching the reactions and the happiness that I can bring to others. It's a fact that I am unable to show much physical affection but in my autistic ways buying and giving enables me to show the people around me how much I love them and care for them.

Child 1 has had the most severe anxiety and nerves with birthdays and Christmas. Christmas Eve and Birthday eve child 1 just couldn't sleep and was up and down all night, usually vomiting from anxiety. It was so sad to see – Christmas and birthdays are supposed to be happy and exciting times. It would upset me, but there was nothing I could do to help. I'd try my hardest to make it all magical and buy the gifts that were wanted, but it just created extreme emotional overload.

Learning and Developing

As touched on in my communication section I find reading overwhelming. For me, I can interpret different types of documents in various ways which can cause me utter confusion. I then have lots and lots of questions that I need answering to make sense of it all. I can also read far too much into things that are simple and straightforward, therefore my learning and development has been a real struggle.

Taking verbal instructions can be equally challenging for me, I can have the same feelings and reactions that I get from reading.

Sometimes rewording the instructions or directions can make all the difference to my understanding. It's often helpful for another person to word it in their way.

When my husband is explaining things to me, he uses my facial expressions as a guide and asks me, 'If I understand' what he's saying, if it's a 'no' from me then we try and work around it. Such as, saying it in a different way or I will ask questions to try and understand what's being said to me. There are times when I just cannot grasp it and when we've exhausted all possibilities, we leave it before a heated debate starts.

It's better for me to have very small and uncomplicated instructions to work with to be able to learn.

I like IKEA instructions, they are easy and uncomplicated; saying that, I have built things incorrectly in the past, due to my interpretation of what I see.

Over recent years I've become aware that the best way for me to learn and develop is by physically being shown what to do, I find it easier to learn by doing.

I can become frustrated and upset with myself if I can't grasp something (a meltdown has been known to happen), which might include getting angry and not wanting to continue and then self-loathing occurs.

I think if I had have known this at school things may have been very different. My school and college grades weren't disastrous, but they weren't the best either (secretly, I really wanted them to be).

How odd is it that I was better at French and German than I was at English?

I secretly I felt like I was a let-down and I desperately wanted to be as smart as some of the others in school.

I hated revising, I struggled so much with concentrating and trying to retain the information. I took advice on the best way to revise, I even used the little revision cards to make small notes, but I just couldn't do it.

The build up to my exams was extreme and I detested it, the time pressure, the reading of the questions and not having a clue what they meant. I would overthink how to answer the questions. I would feel a build-up of emotions to the point of crying.

Leaving the exam room always left me feeling deflated and with a sense of failure.

It's always drilled into you by teachers and schools that 'you must get good grades, in order for you to have a good job' and to have a successful life – absolute BULL SHIT. The schooling system does not suit everyone.

I moved on from secondary school to college and then I planned on attending university.

I had the pre-conceived idea in my head that going to university was the thing you had to do.

I didn't really have a plan, there weren't any subjects I loved, so I just went with the subjects that I did the best in at school.

I kind of hoped that spending another two years studying would enlighten me to which career path to choose.

That didn't happen and I disliked college too.

By the end of college there was no way I could go to university, I couldn't do anymore 'studying', it just wasn't for me. I was then left pondering what I was going to do with my life.

I always felt so lost, most of my school friends (more acquaintances) knew what direction in life they wanted to take, and it felt weird to me knowing I didn't have a frigging clue.

It makes me sad that schools and how they teach is so archaic. Not all children are academic. How many successful people are there in our world that were kicked out of school or left school without any grades? Lots of them.

How many neurodiverse children are there who just cannot handle the current ways of teaching and the system? Lots of them. It's almost as if the non-academic and neurodiverse children are being set-up to fail.

How does this help with confidence, self-esteem, or mental wellbeing? In my opinion, it doesn't. It certainly didn't help me.

I did move on to be self-employed, then I spent around nine months in a small family-run DIY shop (I loathed it). I spent 13 years working in a very well-known supermarket chain. I got promoted twice, and in my last year with the company I moved to a different area within the company. It all ended in a heart breaking and very traumatic way for me. I then took some time to be a full-time mum and I then became self-employed again.

After my diagnosis I realised that there is no way I could return to a normal job. I still feel stuck in life, I try new businesses and give it my all, yet they haven't been too successful, I then spiral into self-doubt, but I really should feel proud of my achievements.

TASK INTERRUPTION

I get really annoyed when I'm doing a task or job and I get interrupted. I get irritated, snap at people, and seem irrational, it's horrible.

When I'm doing a task, I can quickly become deeply involved; I have a list in my head of what I want to achieve and when I want to achieve it by.

Someone may try and talk to me; I hear the noise but don't absorb what is being said. I stop what I'm doing, maybe not straight away.

I try to finish the part that I'm doing before interacting with them but then I can be seen as ignorant.

If I know someone is by my side waiting for me to interact with them, I'm usually unable to continue with my work as my thoughts move to the person standing near me. 'What do they want?', 'Why are they here?', 'What's wrong?', 'Why are they staring at me?'.

After the interruption, I've got to try and pick up where I left off. 'What were my train of thoughts?', 'What was I writing?', 'How do I begin again?', 'I can't be bothered now'.

Mostly, what I was thinking or doing has been completely lost and it's really irritating, it almost feels rude that I was interrupted even when it's not.

At least I know that the train of thoughts will come back as I try and sleep or in the middle of the sodding night!

Did you know?

That task interruption frustration is an autistic thing.

I didn't know, I just thought I was a shitty person for feeling and reacting in an impolite manner.

Hyperfixations/ Hyper Focus

Hyper focus

Definition: The intense focus on one thing to the exclusion of everything else.

Fixation

Definition: An obsessive interest in or feeling about someone or something.

Having a hobby or passion is good and healthy, but these interests can become negative if they take over a person's life or interfere with their relationships. Some last a few weeks, some a few months, some years, some come and go.

If an interest becomes a fixation, they can take over our daily lives very quickly, possibly costing us money, time, or our relationships.

My main fixation has been the gym, I've done it from aged 15 years old and I won't ever stop. I've been in desperate pain, almost unable to walk, but still go.

I do believe that if I hadn't have had this mindset in regard to the gym, my body would be in a bit of a mess.

Growing up I had a 'thing' for teddy bears and stationery. God how I loved stationery, I just thought it was amazing. All those coloured pens and pencils, bright patterned books, the books with different lines inside and the fantastic pencil cases.

During my teenage years my parents took me on holidays to France and in France they have 'Hypermarches' (really big supermarkets). These supermarkets are just incredible and I loved them, they felt so big and sold everything a person could ever need, and lots of things a person didn't really need.

Inside these 'Hypermarches' were multiple aisles of stationery and I was in heaven. I would always buy my back-to-school essentials and felt chuffed not only as I had new and exciting stationery but I knew nobody else would have the same items as me.

Another BIG fixation over the last year was Ancestry. I first joined Ancestry in 2017 and did a bit of family research and got some great results. We even travelled to America to meet newfound relatives.

January 2022 I had a bee in my bonnet and wanted to find out more about my close family history. Within weeks of finding out what I needed, I had already agreed to help another family member with their Ancestry and then another and another.

I am but a novice with it all, but being autistic with a hyperfocus allows me to grow and learn very quickly, with a huge desire to find the answers at any price.

Ancestry is like a puzzle, it's fact finding, and one thing leads to another and another and another, it's never ending.

It quickly became a hyper fixation, it became obsessive; I worked on it whenever I could. Morning, through the day, evening, and night-time. Hour after hour, week after week, month after month.

The help I gave to others I did it for free as I wanted to help but it came at a cost. For a year it's taken over my life.

It negatively interfered with my family life and my work life. It literally took over my life.

I can't regulate the time to spend on projects. All I know is that if something needs achieving or completing, I cannot stop or relax. It takes over my body and brain until it's all done, whatever the cost might be.

Through the Ancestry journey of helping others, I lost sleep, I couldn't fall asleep as my mind was buzzing with theories, how to progress. I would dream about what I was doing night after night. I would wake up and Ancestry was all I could think about and the people I needed to find. It wasn't good.

At points the tiredness, the obsession, the screen time, the headaches, inability to think of nothing else took its toll and made me ill, not just once but multiple times. After finding four unknown biological fathers and unknown families, I knew I had to leave it for a while, even though the fourth search wasn't fully concluded I knew I must stop for my family and my sanity's sake.

The more I analyse myself the more I see. It wasn't until recently that I realised how quickly I get hyper focused.

Me and my husband are currently having to finish our garden renovations after we gave the company we hired for the job the sack. Long story.

It's been a long and tedious seven weeks since they left. One of the jobs that needed doing was to clean the existing brickwork from all the mortar splatted all over it. There's so much brickwork area to clean. My husband ordered a tub of brick acid, brushes, and some gauntlet gloves – this would be one of my jobs. I was nervous at first, but I rapidly got into the swing of it. It's painfully slow to do, the solution is brushed on one brick at a time and then scrubbed in before being washed off with water. I don't think I helped myself as I'm using a paint brush that measures half an inch. The areas I have done so far are looking great, super clean but now all I can think of is to get the rest done. I'm planning when I can do it and how much I can do at any one time.

Having to take over the garden work and getting it finished has become a Hyperfocus. It's not great for my husband as I drone on and on about it, he's only one man doing the job, using holiday days from work and weekends to work on this, but all I see is it's not finished and all the jobs that are left to be done. We are getting there slowly and by mid-summer it SHOULD be completed.

A little while back I was in the hairdressers, and it was time to wash off my colour. My hairdresser motioned to me to go and sit in the special chair with the most uncomfortable neck positioning ever. It's not just this one, they are all the same, wherever I've been.

But what I realised is that once I sense myself feeling uncomfortable, all my brain can do is hyperfocus on what I'm feeling to the point where I have a build-up, become anxious and physically can't stand it anymore, until I move. I want to sit up and lift my head up, but I can't as I'm having my hair washed so I move around just to make it less uncomfortable. When I'm like this no amount of distraction helps me.

I had a similar situation with a full spinal MRI scan once. I've had a few MRI scans and knew what they are and what happens, but I still get anxiety.

I was told the MRI scan would last approximately 45 minutes and you guessed it, I panicked, that's a long time to be in there.

It's not very warm, it's noisy, you have to lie very still, and my face felt close to the top of the scanner. Each and every one of the above became a hyperfocus, my emotions built up so much that my heart rate increased, and almost started to cry so I pressed my button and asked to have a break as I was panicking that much.

The staff were great and turned me around, so my head was sticking out of the machine and my feet were inside it. I settled ok and I had no issue with the remainder of the scan.

I think I have or have had more hyper fixations than I realise. When I sit and think about it there are loads. I go all in and most of it just fizzles out.

I've done this with people too, they show interest in me, I feel a connection with them, and I get all excited that someone could possibly like me and could possibly be my friend. I overshare, I talk about them lots, I'm keen on keeping up contact and then reality kicks in and I start to see them for who they are, not what I thought they were. Or, quite possibly, I'm not a good fit for them either. #embarassing.

Bodybuilding

THE GYM THING.

I'm on a mission, I have a goal.

When I got to 40 years old, I decided (for whatever reason) that I wanted to do a 'fitness model photo shoot'. It would be something that would push me, it would be something well out of my comfort zone, but I wanted to do it.

It never happened, I just plodded on with life, I never took my idea very seriously. I carried on working out, my idea remained inside my head, I thought to myself nice idea, but it will never happen. This was around the time child 1 started with problems too so that was more important than my 'idea'.

Fast forward to the end of 2021 and my 'idea' started to return to the forefront of my mind. By this time, I had my diagnosis, and life was better but I couldn't help but feel a little bit negative, I felt I had let myself down that I hadn't done my photo shoot when I was 40, years had passed, and my weight had fluctuated and I was the heaviest I had been outside pregnancy. Whatever I had lost over the previous years just crept back on and more. This was all new to me as I had always been slim and managed to control my weight.

I took control and told myself to go for the goal, I wanted to do this for me but to also inspire others.

On the first day of March 2022, I started my transformation. I spent six months with a personal trainer, who just wasn't right for what I needed, so I asked for help from someone else. The decision to change was the best decision I could have made.

I thought to myself that going from fat(ish) (in my eyes) to photo fit and defined should be easy. I knew how to train, I just needed someone to guide me on my nutrition and I would be set.

How wrong was I?????

The gym is my ultimate hyper fixation, the one that has been a continual source of help for me, my body, and my mind for 30 years.

At 15 I joined the local gym, with my 'Mr Motivator' multi coloured, Lycra bodysuit (I didn't have the bum bag though), and went on the 'ladies only' days. It was terrifying but I loved it. It became addictive.

My 15 year old self thought that if I went to the gym and changed my body shape, then I wouldn't get bullied at school. Not that I did encounter much bullying; however, I thought it would be a deterrent.

My natural body frame and shape is slender, I was about 5ft 6 ½ – the half is very important. I say was, due to age we all shrink a little bit.

I took my gym training very seriously, loved lifting weights way more than I did the cardio machines.

Over the years I had a few personal trainers, nothing too serious.

I stayed lean but added some muscle but not too much, I always said I looked a little bit athletic. I never aspired to do anything with the way my body looked, it was just to help me feel comfortable and confident. I had lots and lots of comments, other gym users would stare at me and my physique. I would get asked if I competed in bodybuilding – of course I hadn't ever competed in bodybuilding as it terrified me, still does to be fair.

At around 21 years old, I damaged my lower back which would remain , causing all sorts of issues throughout my life.

How did I do it?

I squatted, I did the ass to grass then tried to stand up, I arched my back, my backside stuck out. My lower back felt strange, and I had an uncomfortable feeling, and I didn't like it. I obviously didn't use correct form or technique and therefore sustained an injury.

It wasn't good, sometimes it felt it was the worst pain possible – childbirth is easier. My pain tolerance is fairly low on things that shouldn't really be an issue, yet pushing two humans out of my groin area wasn't too painful. I really don't understand my body.

Due to it being my hyper fixation, I couldn't let the injury I sustained put me off training. I dosed up on pain relief and altered how I trained, worked around my injury. I would cry as there was no relief from the constant pain.

I still suffer today; it's known as chronic pain.

When I was pregnant with child 1, I continued lifting weights until two days before I gave birth. I didn't have anyone telling me how to train when pregnant and I did find it hard to reduce the amount I was lifting and to take time off. I didn't use the internet or any social media, so I just cracked on. I ate super clean, avoided everything that was deemed to be harmful and panicked all the time. My second pregnancy was totally different, but then so was my marriage and my life.

I didn't manage to train as much with my pregnancy with child 2 as I had a few complications, slight bleeding early on and tightening of my womb, so I had to be more careful with what I did.

In my 30 years of gym time, I've been a member of a few gyms. Sometimes, I just couldn't cope in that particular gym anymore, some gyms closed down which meant I had no choice but to move.

Starting in a new gym takes some mental and physical strength and on most days that's just to leave the house.

I've been a member of my current gym from the day they were able to fully open after lockdown. I knew throughout lockdown that I had to find a new gym and it was crazy tough. Once I had located one, I had to endure the build-up and inner strength to actually go. I do quite like it here and I don't intend to move away.

Every day I attend I get the similar anxiety, running through my brain.

> Who's going to be inside?
>
> Who will be the people on reception or stood around the reception desk talking?

I'll just keep my eyes on the floor, fidget around a bit if anyone comes close to me, therefore, I won't have to make any eye contact.

Will I have to make eye contact? Do I feel I can make eye contact today?

Should I just act confident and look at everyone and smile?

Do I wait for them to smile at me?

Will I be able to use the equipment I need to do my workout?

What will I do if I can't do my routine and in the way I normally do it?

The chatting in my brain doesn't stop, I have many questions.

Why have people left weights on the machines?

What are people looking at?

Why do the men use the women's toilet? .

There have been a couple of times that I've refused to use the lady's 'toilette' as some lovely male specimen has done a wee and must have thought their willy was a hose pipe and sprayed like they are watering the plants at home. I moan, the staff clean it and then I'm happy to use it again.

My daily mindset has an impact on how I cope with the gym too. If I'm having an emotional or anxious time then I become more withdrawn and I don't want any form of contact, from anyone. If I've had a good sleep, and feel recharged and relaxed then I can be happy, smily and chatty.

I can imagine what's been said about me. Me with my RBF and stern walk and harsh manner. I do appear to make life hard for anyone to interact with me. This though, could be all in my mind; in fact, it probably is.

Having anyone in the gym that I speak to makes gym life easier, there's a few older men that I chat to, and I find it easy to have a laugh and a talk to. As I wrote in my communication chapter, when the communication barriers are broken down, people see a different me.

Of course, it's always better to smile and say hello, it's just impossible sometimes. I once learned that if you smile at someone they will smile back. I tried it and it works. Try it for yourself, if you're able to, you'll be surprised by the results.

There are the arrogant, cocky ones who I don't want to converse with, but maybe they act that way due to their own insecurities.

Earlier this year child 2 has joined me in the gym and is absolutely loving it. I love it too, it helps with my anxiety of what's happening around me, as I focus on what child 2 is doing. We train hard and have a craic. Bonding time at its finest.

If I have time away from the gym, I get ridiculously anxious about returning, it can make me feel sick. I did try a different gym for a couple of days to train with likeminded people, I thought it would be beneficial for moving forward in my training. NEVER AGAIN, I hated it, I'll stick with my normal gym, the equipment I know, the faces that I'm familiar with and my routine. I'll just have to make sure that I can move forward in my development in my gym.

Sorry, back to the transformation.

I was really nervous about messaging the new personal trainer/coach. I had seen him on stage in 2019 at the one and only bodybuilding competition that I have been to. He was awesome and I followed him on Instagram. He prepped male and female athletes ready for bodybuilding shows so was used to transforming bodies. To do this you have to have in-depth knowledge, experience and understanding.

Writing and sending that Instagram direct message took some strength, then when I had sent it, I re-read it over and over again. How did it sound? How did I come across? Had I overshared? Should I have sent it? Then there was the anticipation of waiting for a response and what do I do if I don't get a response? He won't reply to me. I felt like a little nobody. I thought with the way he looked and running a bodybuilding coaching business he may not take on someone insignificant like me who just wants to do a fitness model photo shoot.

It felt like forever until I got my reply (it wasn't) but YAY, I got a response.

We had a brief exchange of messages and then we chatted on the telephone – can you imagine my body's reactions to 'Give me a call when it's convenient'. I shit myself. I started shaking like a shitting dog, my heart was pounding and sounded so loud, but I had to get the call over and done with. We talked for about 45 minutes, I spoke obscenely quickly, I overshared, I didn't use social cues, talked over him but I felt so positive afterwards.

Let the challenge begin.

Now the training side of things I'm good at, I like to think I know a fair bit, well you do after 30 years of doing something.

Nutrition on the other hand...

In the conversation with my new coach, we talked about my training methods, how often I visited the gym, how much cardio I did and about the food I ate, including my calorie intake.

Straight away he put a plan into action, training five days per week and then there was cardio to do. I would use old school bodybuilding training methods. The reps would be high 2 sets @15 reps, 2 sets @10-12 reps.

Then we talked about my change of diet; I was pooping myself. I had seen TV shows, social media and read magazines about what and how bodybuilders eat, and it scared me shitless.

I didn't feel like a bodybuilder and using the term bodybuilding was weird. All my life, I just told people I lifted weights, weight trained, I never classed myself as a bodybuilder, but I am.

My food pattern had to change BIG time. I sat listening with dread and fear.

Do you have protein powder?

- Yes, Optimum Nutrition Whey, in Chocolate mint. It's the only one I like; I've tried many over the years and end up throwing them away. I can only drink it thick though – if it's too watery, it makes me gag.

Do you like eggs?

- Erm, kind of, though if I eat too many and continually, they make me feel sick.

So, you can eat omelettes?

- Well, yes but occasionally, they can make me feel sick.

Can you eat them with spinach?

- No, don't like spinach unless it's in a pasty with feta cheese.

Peppers?

- Nope.

Tomatoes?

- God, no. Actually, I can eat the tinned ones if they are mixed in with Spaghetti Bolognese but then I pick the tomato lumps out.

Mushrooms?

- Erm, I can tolerate a few if they are fried in oil with onions. Like when I make Fajitas. Or I can eat them in Spaghetti Bolognese.
- I like cheese with Omelettes.

Do you like porridge?

- Yep, I like porridge but only with cold water then microwaved for one minute and ten seconds, then I add cold milk after.

Do you like rice?

- Yep, but only the long grain rice pre-cooked in the white plastic tub from Aldi. The one where you stab airholes into the lid before cooking.

Do you like veg, like the individual frozen veg bags?

- I like tenderstem broccoli, frozen peas, and carrots. Can't eat frozen veg, the texture is horrible, and the watery taste makes me gag. If the veg gets cold, that's another reason to gag.

Can you eat fish?

- Don't like salmon, tuna, prawns, seafood etc, but I don't mind the white, plain cod and I like the fish from the chip shop in batter.

Are you ok with chicken?

- Yes, but only when it's warm, I can't eat cold chicken.

Do you like rice cakes?

- I can tolerate them but it's like eating polystyrene.

Do you like peanut butter?

- God, no.

What about almond butter?

- Is it like peanut butter cos if it is then I won't like it.

It's similar but it's not the same, why don't you try it?

- I say ok, I'll try it, where do I buy it from? Inside I'm thinking, almond butter is going to be as disgusting as peanut butter. To my surprise, it's bloody gorgeous.

Do you like Greek yoghurt?

- Absolutely.

Do you like berries?

- What type of berries?

Blueberries? Blackberries? Raspberries? Strawberries?

- I can do strawberries.

I've never eaten as many strawberries in my life since getting together with my new coach.

Add some frozen berries to your yoghurt and pre training meals!

- I don't like frozen berries, they are watery with a sour taste – no thank you.

Can you imagine what the new coach was thinking?

I was sent a meal plan. It included all six meals and what to eat. FML. I couldn't get my head around it. I have to eat certain foods at certain times of the day.

My teatime meal included salad.

The homemade salad I make and had growing up would consist of lettuce, cucumber, pickled onions, cheese, ham, salad potatoes or a jacket spud with butter. This isn't the type of salad allowed on a bodybuildingmeal plan.

My diet plan allowed me to eat lettuce, peppers, spinach, tomatoes, cucumber, and fat-free dressings.

I fired question after question to my coach. I don't like all this stuff, especially dressings, I don't like any of them, I don't even like tomato sauce, brown sauce, or mayonnaise.

He allowed me to eat lettuce, cucumber, pickled onions, a bit of cheese and I drizzled some garlic infused olive oil onto it all. Without the olive oil, there's no way I could have eaten the salad.

My sixth meal of the day was 125g of Greek yoghurt, 20g of protein powder, 15g of almond butter and 30g of strawberries. It was to all be added together. I don't think so. There's no way I could add chocolate mint powder into the yoghurt mix so I settled on having my protein powder with 100g of water (nice and thick) and the rest in a bowl. The fat-free Greek yoghurt is disgusting, on its own but mixed with almond butter it's YUM, to be honest I constantly want more.

My meal plans have had to change over time – when your body is changing the food has to change to work alongside it. I don't do too well with this. I try and understand the changes which sometimes I struggle with. My first instinct is to panic and send lots of questions to my coach to make sure I'm getting it correct. After a few days I settle in and I'm ok with the changes.

Over the months there has been times when I've had to go to the gym at different times of the day, sometimes training in a morning or sometimes the afternoon. With this I rearrange the six meals so I'm eating my carbs around my training window; sounds easy to others, not for me. I couldn't work out how to do it and I couldn't explain why I didn't understand it to my coach, so I didn't bother him about this (I also felt a bit stupid too) and just did what I thought was best. I just ate my meals as I had been doing (in my routine) and hoped it was working. Two months ago, I did have that lightbulb moment and figured out how to change my meals to suit my gym workouts, it's all good now.

I have been eating omelettes now for ten months, morning and evening. At the start of this my tolerance for omelettes was low. The way I used to cook them like I did pancakes, I would cook them on one side, it would go crispy and then I would flip them and cook the other side until crispy. NOT ANYMORE.

I found a new way to cook them, and I will quite happily eat omelettes forever. I cook one side until a little bit crispy, then I turn one half of the omelette into the centre and then turn the other half into the centre too and cook a bit more so there's no runny egg. This way the inside of the omelette remains a big soft and squidgy. It was the crispy texture on both sides that I didn't like and made me feel sick.

For months now, I've been really happy with my food plan. My food is bland and repetitive but I find it enjoyable.

I won't lie, the process for me has been a tough one.

Towards the end of 2022, my progress was super slow. I was training hard to the point of exhaustion every week; I was becoming run down and felt rough. It was suggested that due to my age (44) that it would be helpful to have my hormone levels checked. It had been mentioned in jest over the past few years that I could be pre-menopausal, but I told my nearest and dearest to piss off. I had been growing grey hairs for many years, but I thought there's no way I'm heading anywhere near menopause at this age.

Panic and anxiety set in again, but I knew I had to do this to see how my body was or wasn't functioning.

I went to my doctors with a list of the certain hormones that I would need checking. When I spoke to the blood nurse, she said we don't check any of them, you'll just get a routine blood test.

As I continued to plead my case the nurse went and spoke to the doctor, which didn't make any difference. I had my bloods done which came back fine and didn't show any indication of pre-menopause, but if I was still concerned, I could speak to the doctor about my symptoms and possibly have HRT.

I really needed to check specific hormones and the only way I could do this was to have a private blood test. Cue some major anxiety.

After about six weeks I managed to purchase a private blood test, and someone would come to my home and take my blood. Cue more emotional upheaval and anxiety.

The results came back within a few days.

I sent a screen shot to my coach and asked if any of the results meant anything to him as I didn't have a clue what it all meant. He asked me to call him immediately.

All my hormones were lower than a snail's belly. My coach said no wonder you're not getting anywhere.

In February this year I started to supplement my hormones to get them back to a normal level for me to carry on achieving my goal.

I was back on the starting blocks, back to square one. I felt deflated and absolutely gutted. I wanted to achieve my goal so much and this was a major setback. I couldn't help looking at others transforming and feeling negative, but that was their journey, and this was mine. I shouldn't and must not compare.

I had made improvements despite my super low hormone levels so all was not lost, and I had to be positive about the future.

This was going to be a long ride and I had to sit tight and enjoy the journey.

As we age, we are expected to accept getting older, accept all the symptoms and all the shit that comes along with it.

Lower hormones greatly affect how our bodies work and the general population have no idea about it. We are not told by anyone, we have to find out for ourselves.

I think if the correct hormone testing was carried out for men and women and individuals were treated appropriately, then there would be fewer health complications, taking some strain away from the NHS. People would be less dependent on uneccessary medication, live healthier and happier lives. But that's just my opinion.

Last week the scales told me that I had lost two stone since the beginning of March 2022. My scales give a total weight loss, they don't show fat loss. If you don't know, guys, fat loss and weight loss are two different things. I can't remember the last time I was this weight.

For me personally it's more about the body recompositing, the transformation to get to my goal and the confidence I gain from the changes.

I don't know how much longer it will take but I won't give up until I get there, no matter what challenges I face.

My Lack of Imagination

Looking back at my early parenting years, I often felt a sense of disappointment, sense of frustration. I'd look at other mums and dads and look at the interaction they had with their children and feel guilty.

I follow Stacey Solomon on social media and watch her TV shows and how she interacts with children is amazing.

MY CHILDREN

Playing let's pretend and being imaginative, I can't do. It makes me so sad that I couldn't be like this with my children. I couldn't play tea-parties, I'd just sit there and drink from the cup and say, 'that's nice', but that would be it. Child 1 had numerous Sylvanian families that included houses and families and playing make believe, I just sat and watched, I couldn't join in. I didn't know how to.

I couldn't play making tents or pretend houses as having the rooms disorganised with items out of place drove me crazy. I couldn't just let myself go and join in; I didn't know how to.

I couldn't make up stories; however, I could read them.

It can't have been much fun for my children.

I know I'm not to blame and now I know there's a reason behind it, but it hasn't made me feel any less shitty about it all. In my head I feel that this is what children need and what they got was a very different parenting style.

In my own childhood I loved colouring but couldn't draw ad hoc, I could draw if I had something to copy. I didn't make up stories or play pretend.

An ex-work colleague of mine once said to me, 'I'm surprised you had kids.' I assumed she was referring to my sparkling personality and the overwhelming sense that she got from me that I have no seemingly 'normal' motherly ways about me. I'm as far away from being mother nature as a person can be. Honestly, I thought that the way to go in life was to meet someone, get engaged, get married and then have children.

I did just that, I had no clue that there were other ways that I could live my life.

However, I do have the ability to be a little bit creative. I've been able to redesign my home (more than once) and I've renovated a couple of houses, but I'm no interior designer. I learn as I go.

I've tried artificial flower arranging – that went ok but I'm no florist and it took a lot of time and concentration. The act of arranging was therapeutic but dealing with customers and online sales was something I couldn't cope with. The anxiety and stress levels were off the scale and unfortunately, I had to close my little business.

WATCHING TV OR FILMS

I'm aware that most films that I watch are made-up stories and I can watch them with no issues; however, I can't watch sci-fi or other things that are just way too 'out there'. I love a good film that is based on true events, like 'Erin Brockovich'.

I do love documentaries about real life crimes, cold cases, and murders. I love hospital programmes, that show surgeons doing their jobs. I love to see A&E TV shows, it enables me to see things that I would always wonder about but wouldn't get the chance to see.

READING

When I do manage to read, the books that I read are autobiographies/biographies, crime stories, military books, like SAS books and other real-life stories.

I can't do the books that are pure fantasy, I have never read a Harry Potter book, Lord of the Rings, or a love story, I've tried but it's a NO from me.

School and the School Run

There's many day-to-day activities that make me uncomfortable, but the school run had to be high up there on the list.

God, I hated it. I'm lucky that child 1 is now at University and Child 2 is halfway through their secondary school education. There are still the parents' evenings to get through though.

Here's the thing with the school run for little old autistic me.

There's the time watching and anticipation to drop off and collect. I need to be on time, I can't set off late, but I don't want to be too early either.

There seems to be the fight for the car parking places. There's always the parents, relatives or guardians that want to secure their favourite parking place as near to the school as possible and will arrive 15-30 minutes before the children are released.

If I wanted a half decent parking spot, I had to join their madness and go earlier than I should have just to park anywhere near the school. There's the dealing with the people who will park, literally 'anywhere', double yellows, on corners, opposite another parked vehicle so you can't drive down the road as it's so narrow. They park and make visibility for other drivers stupidly difficult, and they just don't care. I would be anxious and frustrated; my right and wrong 'brain' is on high alert with all the ridiculous parking.

I figured out the exact time I needed to get out of the car to get to the school ready for the mass exodus.

Next step: Walking to the school, why was it so uncomfortable for me? Maybe it's having to come into close contact with dozens of other adults, all swarming and gathering.

My anxiety would build, as there are so many parents keen to collect their children. There are the cliques of parents, which made me even more uneasy and awkward. I'd walk towards the area where my child's classroom was and in the hope that nobody would look at me and I wouldn't have to make eye contact or speak. I'd stand all uneasy and I suppose a bit twitchy just waiting for my child to be released. The agony was prolonged when my child was one of the last kids out of school, I just needed to get back to the car, where I could breathe a sigh of relief.

At the time I hadn't been diagnosed with ASD; some days I could look at other people, smile and engage but most of the time I just couldn't do it, I didn't want to be seen by anyone. I often wondered if the other parents noticed and what did they think of my inconsistent behaviour.

Conversing in small talk was just very, very awkward.

Although it was a daily routine, it was unpredictable. There could be last minute changes from within the school, they may want to talk to me, I may have to talk to them. The faces in the school grounds would change daily.

Having to approach the teachers at school about an issue with my children made my already struggling mind and body go up another level. I would have played over the scenario and conversation multiple times, built myself.

Sometimes there would have been conversations with the teachers with no warning, which equally sent me into blind panic.

One day Child 2 brought out a 'special mention' for doing something great. I looked at it and the name had been spelt incorrectly. Not a big deal to some, but for me I wasn't happy. I had brought this to their attention many times and by this point child 2 had been with them nearly five years. I decided to pay the office a visit where three members of staff, including the deputy head, were sitting. I showed them the 'special mention' and said a few words. At this point the deputy head turned and directly spoke to child 2 saying child 2 should have spoken up when it was handed out, putting the blame on child 2. I saw red and raised my voice: 'child 2 is seven and has been here four years, child 2 is a 'child' and it's your responsibility not child 2's'.

Secondary school has had many issues too but luckily you don't have to see the teachers face to face unless it's for parents evening or for award ceremonies. I do still have the anxiety build up when something must be dealt with and I have to make contact with someone.

Child 1 and 2 have to wear special insoles in their shoes. These conditions have been diagnosed by the hospital.

Fitting the orthotic insoles into normal shoes can be a real challenge so we had to find alternative footwear that were comfortable, that fitted in somewhat with the school uniform policy.

There was once a trip to a brewery that child 1 was going on with school and child 1 came home one day and said a teacher had told them the footwear wasn't suitable and if child 1 didn't wear another pair of shoes they wouldn't be going on the trip. Out came my usual response – disbelief, frowning and swearing. The shoes child 1 wore were high top, full leather, all black converse and I mean all black not a dot of another colour. I saw red. I decided to research the brewery to see if there were any specifications on clothing and footwear: nothing. I telephoned the brewery and reiterated what the school had said, I was told by the brewery that there was a lot of walking so the footwear needed to be suitable for that but nothing else.

After I had I called the Brewery, I telephoned the school and asked to speak to the teacher and to ask them why the footwear child 1 was wearing wasn't suitable for the trip. I asked if it was a rule given by the Brewery. The teacher didn't know what to say to me after I told her I had telephoned the Brewery myself for confirmation. Child 1 did visit the Brewery with school and continued to wear the Converse all through school.

Hierarchy and Celebrities

People are people to me, regardless of their rank or superiority, regardless of their status and wealth.

I really don't get it. I don't understand the ordinary public crying over celebrities, they don't know these people personally. They may have seen them on TV or on social media, but how can the public become so attached? How can they throw their underwear at them, what even is that?

I've seen a few celebrities up close, and I don't run to them or hound them. My response is that they are people trying to get on with their daily business, so let them be. I once met a famous husband and wife duo on an inflatable bouncer in the Caribbean Sea. We looked and said hello, then carried on with our thing whilst they did theirs.

I've actually read that us autistic folk seek to be on a level with everyone we meet. Autistics don't recognise authority as a thing in or of itself. We are more likely to be impressed by those around us that have more knowledge, experience, or have good ethics or morals. I'm one of those people.

Autistics don't share the Neurotypical view of authority. Neurotypical people happily accept it and we tend to disregard it.

I remember one incident and I think it sticks in my brain due to it being so wrong, but I didn't know it was wrong at the time. I thought it was comical and the level of seniority never came into play.

In one of my jobs, we used to have a really cool area manager, which in my place of work was quite a senior position. I got on well with the person, I felt relaxed, had a laugh, and banter would quite often take place between us. One day I had to put some paperwork into their drawer, and I wrote a message onto the paper and finished it with,

'Muchos Gracias Penis, thank you very much cock'.

I was amused with myself, laughing at what I'd written and then in the days afterwards the reality kicked in and I felt that nauseous feeling and the embarrassment of what I'd done. These people were in a senior position to me, but I didn't act like it. I sometimes couldn't differentiate the levels of seniority, to me they are just another person in a different job role.

My colleagues would be like, 'shit, the area manager's here' and get all panicky. I'd be like 'and...'.

We'd also have visits from some of the big wigs and everyone used to get their knickers in a twist. We would be told weeks in advance and would have to get the place ready for the visit. More man hours were used, everything had to be cleaned to an inch of its life, it was like a royal visit was taking place, and I didn't get it. I'd always think it's 'much ado about nothing'. In my eyes the MDs (Managing Directors) were arriving to see something fake, it was pretence, and it wasn't the norm, and I always thought that they needed to see what normal was, not anything fake.

People's actions and words changed around the very senior people too, which in turn made me uncomfortable. I'd think to myself, 'Just be normal'. These high-ranking people would be followed around like sheep in their flock.

If I was spoken to most of the time, I had to really think about how to respond. I had to be careful not to do my brutally honest thing, or swear, or start telling them their hair was out of place, or that they had the wrong colour socks on for the suit they were wearing, or cracking a sarcastic joke.

I couldn't have ever joined the forces, having someone volatile in front of you shouting, spitting and swearing in my face. If I see it on TV, it really unsettles me (yep this was a random sentence, lol).

There's been times when we have stayed in some lovely hotels and eaten in some lovely restaurants and the staff are trained very well and we are addressed as Sir/Madam. We have to politely ask them to not do that, it's rather uncomfortable and it's just not us.

A special birthday happened about 13.5 years ago, and it had been a wish to dine in a Michelin star restaurant (also well before I knew I was autistic).

I think at the time Gordon Ramsey was 'the chef, the man' on TV so I decided to book one of his restaurants as a surprise. It was in London, looked very fine and very expensive. I booked it and a night away. It was all very exciting and sounded amazing too, but the reality was different.

1. It served mostly seafood. I don't like seafood; in fact, when we arrived, I didn't like anything on the menu apart from the numerous types of fresh baked bread. For all those wondering, I never checked the menu before booking.
2. It was a very 'Sir and Madam' place.

3. It was a tiny, tiny venue making the closeness of tables an issue for me and the noise.
4. It had a lot of high-flying businesspeople dining.
5. Being from Yorkshire and working class, we really felt uncomfortable.
6. The wine menu was like a novel and prices ranged from £50 upwards to thousands of pounds.
7. I was close to meltdown all night from the minute we arrived.
8. It cost £438 for a meal for two with wine.
9. The best thing about the night was leaving.

It all just feels a bit superficial and awkward. I get upset seeing people bowing down to people and it seemingly showing that some are better than others.

Being Fake, Insincerity, Brown Nosing, Arrogance, Cockiness

Attention, if any of the above refers to you, please stay away, lol.

In my opinion all the above are definitions of people who are not in the realms of reality, they too are masking but not necessarily in the same way as I have masked.

ARROGANCE

- having or revealing an exaggerated sense of one's own importance or abilities:

INSINCERITY

- the quality of not expressing genuine feelings:

BROWN NOSING

- To try too hard to please someone, especially someone in a position of authority, in a way that other people find unpleasant.

COCKINESS

- conceited or confident in a bold or cheeky way:
- conceited – excessively proud of oneself; vain:

FAKE

- not genuine; imitation.

I can't bear it. Fake, falseness, phoniness, and insincerity stand out a mile and I'm not one to hang around, I'd rather not be in their presence. I mean I'm not rude and will stay in the conversation or around the person(s), but in my head I'm thinking all sorts about what they are saying to me whilst I'm politely engaging.

Fortunately, or unfortunately, I do not have a poker face and my eyes and face will express exactly what I'm thinking or feeling. It can be amusing to the people who know me when I'm listening to the hooomans that are full of bullshit as my reactions are well, unpredictable.

As soon as is possible, I'm like, 'where's the exit, please?' or thinking how can I get out of this?

Brown nosing makes me cringe.

Arrogance and cockiness just get me irked.

I'm proud to admit that I don't conform to these traits, I'm honest and real. Maybe, a bit too honest and real for some, and maybe, that's why I'm seen as a bit of a 'Marmite' character – you like me, or you don't, there's no in-between.

Emergency Situations

I've come to realise that in pressured situations, non-planned situations and when I'm overloaded, I don't respond very well. My adrenalin kicks in quickly, my mind goes into overdrive and masses of thoughts flood my brain and I feel out of control.

But yet, I am thankful and blessed to be autistic, if it wasn't for my overthinking, my catastrophising, my overactive thoughts, my fretfulness, my anxiousness, the following situations could have been very different.

2018.

Child 1 started to have problems walking; the right leg was doing some strange movements; the right knee would head off on its own towards the left knee and they would nearly clash. The right knee started to give way, causing child 1 to drop to the floor without warning and there was no explanation for it. Our local children's hospital couldn't find the cause, an MRI scan showed a double break in the lower back and was deemed not to be the cause. Physio was given but wasn't much use. The problem became that bad that crutches were used most of the time and a wheelchair when it got tremendously tough. My brain went into overdrive, I was watching my child suffer, medical professionals couldn't find what was wrong.

I needed to do something.

One day I was in my hairdresser's, and we were chatting away, catching up on recent events and life stories. I remember her talking about her MS, she talked about the problems she was having, I asked my usual three million questions on how it works, etc.

It started to make me wonder.

I decided to do a 'Dr Google' search on the brain, MS and other possible neurological conditions that may affect signals from the brain to the legs.

I became hyper focused that child 1 needed a brain scan as there was a possibility that the leg problem was neurological. I told the doctors what I thought, and they agreed to do a brain scan. The brain scan was to be done at the same time as a follow up MRI scan of the lower back.

The spinal consultant had good news that the spine wasn't showing any breaks, the break had healed, but something had been found in child 1's brain on the MRI scan. Me and child 1 looked at each other and cried. The doctor told us it was an AVM (Arteriovenous Malformation); he couldn't tell us anymore as he was a spinal doctor not a neurologist.

I thought FML, you receive some shitty news, but you'll have to wait a few weeks to find out any details. Dr Google was on hand to help (or make us feel worse) about what a cerebral AVM was.

'A brain AVM is a tangle of abnormal and poorly developed blood vessels connecting arteries to veins. AVMs are rare and occur in less than 1% of the population.

In normal situations arteries take oxygen rich blood away from the heart to various parts of the body under high pressure and so have strong muscular walls.

We were knocked sick at this point, child 1 just kept having some serious medical issues.

The most common complications of AVMs are bleeding and seizures, the bleeding can cause significant neurological damage and may be fatal.

AVMs are either found by accident or when there has been a brain haemorrhage. This was some serious shit.

The neurologist told us that if left untreated the risk of the brain bleed throughout child 1's life was very, very high and would be life-altering or fatal. We knew that the AVM had to be dealt with.

We were presented with two options.

Option 1 would be to cut open and remove part of the skull and then the AVM is surgically removed.

Option 2 would be Stereotactic Radiosurgery. This is a non-invasive treatment to deal with the AVM. A cerebral angiogram is done to localise the AVM, focus beam, high energy sources are concentrated on the AVM which damages the vessels, produce scarring and the AVM then dries up.

Option 1 carries more risks, but it's all dealt with quickly.

Option 2 is a long and drawn-out process. We were told that it could take between two to four years for the AVM to close and in that time, there are still risks from a live AVM. There also could be swelling around the brain from the SRS causing its own problems.

Child 1 wanted option 2 and the consultant agreed that at 15 years of age it was a safer option too.

The SRS went great, and the AVM responded well. Swelling in the brain did occur, which wasn't pleasant, for which medication was given that in turn caused hallucinations and other symptoms.

As I write this, we are four years on from the SRS and at the last MRI the AVM had almost been obliterated. We are currently waiting for the last angiogram later this year to confirm obliteration.

Fingers crossed.

MARCH 2020 JUST BEFORE THE FIRST LOCKDOWN.

I was asked by my parents if I would mind picking them up from our local train station as they returned home from India.

I turned up to meet them, with child 2. On approach to the car my mum was walking slowly and didn't seem happy. When they got into the car my dad said Mum wasn't very well and hadn't been the whole trip home. Mum was insistent that she was fine, just tired, needed to go home and needed her bed.

My dad kept saying she wasn't fine.

I noticed her breathing was laboured and shallow. I decided to not drive them home but took them straight to our local hospital A&E department, I knew they were both tired, but this seemed important.

Mum was having a heart attack. I couldn't believe it; my mum was fit and healthy; it didn't make sense. It turned out not to be the usual heart attack, but a heart attack caused by micro vascular angina. Mum's fully medicated now and fully better.

JUNE 2023

My parents were going on one of their annual holidays, it was a much-needed break for them. It had been meticulously planned for a long time. They were due to travel to the airport by train, an easier and cheaper option with less hassle.

A few weeks before, there were rail strikes and their train was cancelled. My dad asked me If I would take them to the airport. I said yes, no problem. We would set off in plenty of time and would take the scenic route to avoid traffic and the views would be nicer. My parents have driven this way a few times and my dad had his little list of towns/villages that we pass through just in case we needed it. My dad sat in the passenger seat, child 2 was behind me and my mum sat behind my dad.

I'm a confident driver and don't get fazed by much.

We left mid-morning, thinking traffic would be ok and the journey would be a breeze, but about 30 minutes in, the traffic build up started and we encountered lots of roadworks. We were about two-thirds of the way to the airport when I noticed that my dad was getting a little uneasy (his body language changed). He said he didn't recognise the roads or places that we were driving through and so we must have gone wrong. My dad is a very experienced driver, having driven as a professional at times, he's well-travelled and knows routes. So, when he said he didn't recognise where we were, I thought we must have gone wrong.

My mum got Google Maps on her phone and my dad started to look at his phone. Mum said, yes we were on the right road and right at that minute we saw the next village which was on my dad's list. We came up against more traffic hold ups which was delaying us slightly, but we would still reach the airport in plenty of time. The sat nav arrival time was around 12:15. At this point dad was still acting uneasy and I asked him what his flight time was – he responded '12:40'. I frowned and looked at him and said it can't be, we won't get to the airport until 12:15 at the earliest. He then said they were flying at something past 11. I said, 'are you sure you've got the right time, Dad? If not, you're going to miss your flight?' My parents are frequent travellers and their organisational skills with travelling are second to none. My mum interjected and said the flight was around 14:40, I was a tad relieved. My dad was then trying frantically to use his phone but kept saying, 'it's not letting me, it's not doing it', he repeated it over and over. I said, 'Dad, it might be that there's no signal around here.'

I then asked child 2 to take my dad's phone and to hot spot it so he could get some sort of signal and then Dad could do whatever he was trying to do.

My dad managed to open the easyJet app and look at his flight details, he then said, 'it's not telling me'. I said, 'Dad, what isn't it telling you?' He repeated the same words. I took his phone and said to him, 'It says, your flight is at 14:45.' Dad continued tapping on his phone screen and said, 'It's not doing it, it's not telling me.' I asked him again, 'What isn't it telling you?' I took his phone again and said, 'Dad, it says your flight is at 14:45 and you land at 21:00.' He took the phone and was tapping on the QR code as if it would do something.

I told him that tapping on that QR code wasn't working. It was out of character and odd. My dad's a very smart, clued-up Yorkshire man with no ailments or problems. It was a hot sunny day, so I told him to have a drink. He replied that he didn't want one. I said, 'Dad, please have a drink.' I offered him some chocolate as I thought his sugar levels may have dropped (he isn't diabetic, but I thought it might help); he refused. This was odd as Dad has the sweetest tooth imaginable and he's a bit of a gannet. I turned and glanced at Mum and we both frowned at each other, signalling that something wasn't right.

We were getting closer to the airport and Dad was still speaking and acting oddly. For whatever reason, I said to Dad, 'What I'm going to ask you might sound a bit strange, but what's your name?' He chuckled, was a bit twitchy and didn't answer. Mum is sat in the back now panicking and loudly interjects with, 'what's your name?'. I motioned to her to quieten down. I asked again, 'Dad, what's your name?' His reply was, 'I'll tell you in a minute.' Mum shouts again in a very agitated state, 'PETER, WHAT'S YOUR NAME?' In my head I'm thinking Mum you've just told him. He said his name was Peter but couldn't say his full name. I asked him, 'Dad, when were you born?' I got nothing. At that point I said he needs medical attention; he's having a stroke. My mum carried on asking him questions he couldn't answer, he knew he was going to the airport and knew which terminal he was flying from, but didn't know where his destination was. Some of his words were slurred and he was incoherent, but at the same time was getting frustrated and hostile.

At the point when I realised Dad was having a stroke, my adrenalin and anxiety kicked in. I had never been around anyone who had suffered a stroke, and this was happening to my dad. I felt like I didn't know what to do. In a raised voice, I told Mum and child 2 to ring 999.

999 told us to pull over, I had just entered a motorway, so I wasn't doing that, they advised me to come off the motorway and sit

and wait for them. I knew the airport wasn't too far away and for some reason I knew that reaching the airport would be the best and safest option to get help. I knew that there would be immediate help if I reached the airport. 999 advised us to get to the nearest hospital. As they were speaking, I was trying to type the nearest hospital into the sat nav. I was trying to drive on unfamiliar roads, trying to concentrate on my driving, I was dealing with my dad (who was quite aggressive at the time), who was threatening to get out of the car, while it was moving and I was trying to take in what was being said by the 999 call handler.

The call handler asked to speak to my dad and when he was handed the mobile phone, he hung up on them. I couldn't believe it – my dad talks to anyone, he's so chatty and in a normal situation would never hang up on medical professionals.

I was struggling to type the hospital name into the sat nav, I kept spelling the name wrong, so I let out a frustrated and emotional outburst and I started to go into meltdown. Right at that point I saw the exit sign for the airport and felt the tiniest bit of relief. My dad kept pointing to Terminal 1 but I had seen a police van and I knew I needed to stop him to get help. At that point my dad was getting angry that I wasn't going to Terminal 1 and again threatened to get out of my moving car on the roundabout. Within a minute, I had managed to jump out of my car and stop the police officer, I rambled on in my shaky state that I thought my dad was having a stroke and we needed some help. My dad had got out the car and when the police officer spoke to him, he was still incoherent.

I rang my voice of reason, shaking, crying and with a raised voice and remember saying my dad was having a stroke but then I can't remember anything else of the conversation.

We were instructed to get back in my car and follow him just around the corner to the airport police station.

It was literally just around the corner; I dumped the car behind the police van. I was still frantic. By the time I had exited my car my dad had jumped out too followed by my mum and child 2. As if by magic, instantly there were two armed police officers stood by us plus the first police employee that I had flagged down.

One of the armed police concentrated on my dad, the other on me. It wasn't long before a paramedic arrived on the scene, then airport staff and then we heard blue lights of the ambulance and then another three armed police. They were all so calm and amazing, and it's what my frantic, panicked, autistic ass needed.

I just knew that getting to the airport was the right thing to do and it was, help was instant, and we were so lucky.

I carry a Police and Emergency services autism card with me for such situations but forgot to show it, DOH!

We were told that dad had suffered a TIA (a mini stroke), the holiday was postponed until tests and medication were sorted out, much to my dad's annoyance. He felt ok, didn't see what all the fuss was about.

A TIA is sometimes an indication of a major stroke or more mini strokes. Dad needed to have some tests and needed to be put on preventative medication. So, for the following days and week after the TIA we were on high alert. Exactly one week after the TIA, I drove them back to the airport where they flew out and enjoyed their holiday.

As much as I find my autistic brain a pain in the ass, like last night I couldn't fall asleep as it wanted to ruminate and loop over nothing important, I feel truly blessed in times like these.

Myths About Autism

Autistic people don't understand sarcasm.

I grew up around sarcasm and banter, I understand some sarcasm and use it quite a lot. There are a few occasions when I'm unsure whether to take the individual I'm talking to as serious.

My husband is so dry, witty, sarcastic and can instantly blurt out funny things; it's not a talent I share but I wish I did.

Autistic people are geniuses when it comes to maths, we're all like Rain Man.

I laugh at this; my maths skills are shocking. I passed GCSE maths with what was a 'D ' grade, but I resat it at college and achieved a 'B'. It's a good job we have calculators on our phones; even then when it comes to percentages, I'm screwed.

Measurements are the worst thing; I cannot measure, I don't understand it and I can't read a tape measure. I'll say it's 4", 2/3 and 3 of them sticks, my husband laughs and normally passes a sarcastic comment.

I am pretty good with cars and number plates. I often say to whoever I'm with, 'you see that car, they live at such and such a place'.

I can recite number plates, my bank account numbers, card numbers too including expiry dates and codes. I also remember phone numbers, I still know a mobile phone number from 25 years ago.

You don't look Autistic.

Hang on a minute while I go in the phone box and do a Clark Kent and I'll come back out looking Autistic.

Are autistic people supposed to look a certain way?

Autism is a mental health condition.

No, no, no and more no. Our brains just work in a different way.

Mental health conditions are you as a person with add ons like stress, anxiety, and depression. These can all be treated and helped with counselling and/or medication.

There was a time when I escalated a problem I had with a company, and I asked to speak with an actual person as it would be easier. As we spoke, I told the person how the situation was affecting me and that I was autistic. The response was 'she understood as she had previously worked with people with mental health issues' – Really!

People who are autistic can't show emotion.

Oh yes, we can, it might not be what's classed as a typical show of emotion but it's still there.

Autistic people are all the same.

As autistic people we are still individuals, we all have different hair styles and colours, different eyes, different sized feet, a love for different hobbies and interests. All our strengths and weaknesses are very different.

No two NT (Neurotypical) humans are the same so why should people with Autism all be the same?

I have expert knowledge on this fact.

I'm autistic, Child 1 is autistic, we may have similarities, but we are so very different.

You can't be autistic; you make eye contact.

Years of practice.

You can't be autistic, you're female.

Oh dear. Yes, it's a fact that both male and females can be autistic.

Boys with characteristics of autism are likely to be identified by parents, teachers, or professionals earlier on in their childhood than females.

Autistic females may not fit the commonly accepted profile of an autistic person; therefore, many receive their diagnosis much later than boys.

Only children have autism.

Does autism mysteriously vanish when you reach puberty?

I'm living proof that adults have autism too.

All autistics take things literally.

Nope that will be kleptomaniacs.

The list is endless...

People need to be enlightened.

We need more awareness, with a bit more awareness and then a huge dollop of awareness thrown in for good measure.

Lack of Help

In my opinion and from my experiences, there are a select few who fully understand about autism.

As an adult the moment you learn you're autistic, the help and support are non-existent. I was completely floored to learn there would be no other help available for me and child 1 post-diagnosis. Each of us received a single one-hour follow up appointment which allowed us to talk through our results and to have any of our questions answered, but that was it. I asked the person who did my follow up appointment what happens next? Where do I go from here? And the answer was, there's nothing else.

It was all new to me and child 1, we didn't have any known autistics in our family life, what we knew was very limited. I know for sure that if we hadn't have done our own research, we would still be uneducated.

How many autistic adults are unable to research or have support to help them understand about themselves?

I feel the lack of awareness regarding ASD is everywhere in our society – if people are uneducated how can we expect them to understand or help us when it's needed?

In general, companies large and small don't train their staff in autism, and therefore are unable to communicate in the correct manner with anyone that is. There is also the stigma that is associated with autism, misconceptions, stereotyping, avoidance, discrimination, and general negative attitudes.

There are countless employees working in jobs that are undiagnosed and find it extremely difficult, just like I did.

There are numerous autistic people that won't be employed because they are 'autistic'. It's such a shame as we have so many qualities and skills that are invaluable.

There are people and companies who have dismissed my autism, completely ignoring it.

I've been viewed as a nut job; I can be seen in the outside world as mentally unstable and it's a hard pill to swallow.

One time I was sent to the A&E department by my doctor to get my leg checked out; it was unplanned. I was instantly worried, my emotions were all over the place, anxiety and stress levels were high. I walked into the unfamiliar A&E department which was full to bursting. The seats are positioned so that they are facing the reception desk, so all eyes were on me, and everyone could hear what I was saying. I was overcome by the lights, the sounds, and smells. I booked in with the lady on reception and asked if there was a room I could sit in away from the main reception as I'm autistic. I presented my special card to prove that I'm autistic, not that I should need to, but I feel like I need to be believed as I 'don't look autistic'. I was astounded by the response. I was told there was nowhere quiet for me to wait but I could go and stand outside and wait and someone would come and get me when it was my turn to be seen. It was cold and dark, the waiting times were over four hours, I was there over six.

'So, I went and happily stood outside for six hours and froze my tits off'. Obviously, I didn't as I don't like being cold. I felt extremely angry and upset but just had to suck it up and deal with it.

Autism is still seen by many to be a mental illness, and this drives me crackers. Before mine and child 1's diagnosis, I ignorantly asked child 1's psychologist what was the difference between ASD and mental health.

Her response has stuck with me.

Imagine you as a person, mental health issues are you as a person with things added on to you, like stress, anxiety, depression. These problems can be treated either by counselling or by medication and they can (not always) go away.

Autism is you as a person, your brain is hardwired differently. Nothing can be added or taken away. Autism cannot be treated or medicated, it's who you are.

What I was hearing floored me, in a good way.

My brain wiring isn't a choice. My autism isn't a choice.

Final Words

It's only a few years on from my Diagnosis and I'm still learning, I've learned some new things whilst writing my book too and that's Super, Smashing, Great.

I don't think I will ever fully be understood, not even by my own family, but that's ok.

As a family we do our best to face the daily challenges and there will always be ups and downs.

I'm massively grateful for my small and fantastic support system, I don't know where I'd be without them all.

I still find everyday life extremely difficult, but with my fantastic family around me it's all manageable.

Getting older helps too, I have become a little bit wiser and have more drive and desire to keep moving onwards and upwards.

More and more TV documentaries are being produced regarding autism. There are more celebrities spreading awareness, more social media groups and content being shared, and more people than ever are being diagnosed as autistic.

I'm hoping that by sharing my book that I too am contributing to creating more awareness and understanding of what life as an autistic adult is like.

The world has so much more to do to accommodate ND people but it's slowly moving in the right direction. We all make the world a better place.

Please, please, please always remember.

BE BOLD, BE BEAUTIFUL, BE DIFFERENT, BE YOU.

Giving Thanks

MY FAMILY

MUM AND DAD

I'd like to thank my mum and dad for creating me and giving me life. For their unconditional love, for raising me, being there for me, and for giving me everything I needed.

TO MY HUSBAND

From the day we met you have made me feel safe and protected in a way that I have never felt before. You opened my eyes, positively changed my life and have loved me unconditionally. You are my strength, my support, my everything, my sarcastic asshole who makes me laugh and cry at the same time. It's not been easy for us but we are the happiest we have ever been.

I cannot imagine what life would have been like for me if we hadn't met that night.

CHILD 1

We have been on such a journey; it's been a struggle, but we have grown together to create an unbreakable bond.

You are a beautiful person. You have overcome so much in your life already and you are incredible. You have shown strength that I could only ever dream of having.

You have taught me so much and if it wasn't for you, we would never have known we were autistic. Your life is yours to grab, take hold of and enjoy, enjoy everything you can. Grab those opportunities and go for it, never look back and never regret anything.

CHILD 2

My gorgeous, incredible child 2, you made me feel love in a way I never thought possible and emotions that I didn't know I had. You are a gorgeous human inside and out, you're talented beyond belief and I want you to realise it, have faith, have confidence and you'll be unstoppable. I know whatever you do you will be happy; and I will be by your side whenever you need me.

I love you all.

More thank yous

I would also like to thank my coach – Danny Ingram (Find him on Instagram or Facebook). My body has changed so much. I have achieved more with my body with your coaching than I have ever done in my life.

I'm looking forward to what's coming next, let the journey continue.

My wacky, weird, fun, and entertaining Saxophone tutor, Mark Archer (Blowout Sax), an incredible musician. Thanks for your knowledge, your skills, your teaching and our shared love of music and indeed the Saxophone.

Thank you, Lauren, at Inkandpixel@hotmail.co.uk for my cracking illustrations.

Abbreviations

Arse – Bum/Bottom

ASD – Autistic Spectrum Disorder

AVM – Arteriovenous Malformation

Cack – Rubbish

CBT – Cognitive Behavioural Therapy

Does my head in – Drives me crazy, upsets me

FFS – For fuck's sake

FML – Fuck my life

Fuck off Karen – Go away, you annoying person

FYI – For your information

Gets on my tits – Frustrates me

Gets on my wick – Annoys me

Giddy – Happy, excited

Hubbie/Hubster – Husband

Muttley laugh – Muttley is a fictional cartoon character from the TV show, Wacky Rraces.

My voice of reason – Husband

ND – Neurodiverse / Neurodivergent

Not giving a monkeys – Not caring

Nowt – Nothing

NT – Neurotypical

Plonker – Idiot

PTSD – Post Traumatic Stress Disorder

Shit – Oh no, Oops, Uh-oh

Squidge – cuddle

SRS – Stereotactic Radiosurgery

Tit – Slang word for silly, make an idiot of myself

Tizzy – State of confusion, anxiety or excitement

VPL – Visible panty line

WTF/WTAF – What the fuck/what the actual fuck

www.ingramcontent.com/pod-product-compliance
Lightning Source LLC
LaVergne TN
LVHW012044160826
845678LV00014B/2693

* 9 7 8 1 9 1 6 5 7 2 5 6 0 *